Ken Kern
Steve Magers

FIRE

PLACES
SPACES

CHARLES SCRIBNER'S SONS
NEW YORK

Charles Scribner's Sons
New York

We are grateful for the help of:

Barbara Kern, our editor, who typed and retyped this manuscript many times,

Lynn Walters, for her enthusiasm, not to mention her photos and helpful suggestions,

Michael Eckerman, whose photography and masonry skills have contributed much to the contents.

Contents

Introduction

In the past decade, we have seen a dwindling of world energy supplies and the revival of wood as a fuel for home heating. The reason is hardly mysterious, for wood is a renewable, non-toxic resource, available to many simply for its cultivation and harvest. Another restoration in this era of shortages is the long dormant technology of woodstove design, which has recently been reinstated to a position of prominence. Unfortunately, the image of the fireplace as a viable means of efficient heat production suffers from the stigma of wastefulness. The traditional fireplace not only sends some 80 percent of the fire's heat up the chimney but a goodly portion of the room's heat as well.

Numbers, however, are not the measure of all values. The incalculable, age-old appeal of the open fire cannot be plugged into an equation which yields a figure for thermal-units-per-hour. It is just as true that the fireplace is often the center of the home around which a family gathers to share a kind of warmth not provided by even the most efficient woodstove. For years we authors have been researching and experimenting with fireplace design in an attempt to strike a satisfactory balance between preserving the mystique of the open fire and using wood fuel to its best advantage.

In this respect, a review of the literature on fireplace design and building is disappointing. The fireplace is most often presented as a decorative adjunct to home ornamentation. Its value is seen largely in terms of its appeal as a "focal point" or a "conversation piece" for home decor. The possibility that a fireplace can function as a reliable source of household heat is ignored.

It was not until 1969 that the 17th century work of Count Rumford was at last popularized by Vrest Orton in his book, **The Forgotten Art of Building a Good Fireplace**. In his restatement of Rumford's principles, Orton revives the idea that, when correctly built, a fireplace can be a major source of home heat. This is, however, a theoretical book, dealing more with basic concepts than the specifics of fireplace construction.

In our book, we will explore the principles of heating with wood, and we will offer details for fireplace design. We have included step-by-step procedures for building both all-masonry and metal-jacketed fireplaces, and we will explore heat distribution by radiation, convection, and conduction. Finally, we will expand the concept of the fireplace to one of its functions as an integral part of the home, or **firespace**, as we choose to call it.

The concept of the firespace did not originate with us. It had its origin in the Middle

Ages, when the fireplace was enclosed with side walls and crowned with an immense hood. Those tending the fire stood within this hooded area, where they also tended the cooking pots and the roasting spit. A kind of room-within-a-room, this cooking area became known as the "chimney corner."

In his book on the history of fireplaces, John Ruskin, the 19th century art historian, remarks that this cozy, if somewhat smoky, space "had its charms on cold, raw nights and when quiet gossip had to be exchanged, so the placing of a settee against the inner side wall came about, and then the host and hostess assumed the privilege of occupying these seats, sitting sociably side by side on

benches on opposite sides of the hearth. Here confidences were exchanged, grave counsel debated, and light gossip indulged in. It provided the privy cabinet just away from the domestic forum of the hall."

Even after cooking ceased to be a primary function of the fireplace, the chimney corner survived as a place of social gathering in the farmhouses and inns of Renaissance Europe. Partitions separated the commons area from the small, private firespace, called the "ingle nook," which is Gaelic for fire corner. This area was often embellished with carved screens and square or semi-circular windows set in on either side.

Today, this former arrangement is preserved in our contemporary design, where the entire house functions integrally with its wood-burning core, distributing and storing heat and providing the companionable atmosphere of the open hearth. Details are to be found in our last chapter.

Implicit in our concept of the firespace is the present universal awareness that any fuel — or any resource, for that matter — is not ours for casual squander. The notion that we may continue to erect ever larger houses that are continuously heated by wasteful devices is an obsolete indulgence. As in the past, when the fireplace warmed those closely grouped about its opening, the firespace of today can serve the enduring human need for emotional as well as bodily warmth.

Fireplace Development

Perhaps it was the cave dweller who first discovered fire and its uses. In France, evidence from one prehistoric cave indicates that early man was aware of three essential ingredients for firemaking: adequate air (or oxygen), minimum kinling temperature, and volatile fuel. Within this cave, a number of centrally located, circular, stone-lined hearths were found. Their central location suggests to anthropologists that the fire builder was concerned with supplying sufficient draft (air) to the fire from all sides. The size of the hearth was proportional to the probable fuel supply, accomodating both quick-starting kindling and long-burning logs. The cave dweller apparently discovered that greater burning temperatures could be reached by placing a bank of stones around the perimeter of the fire. As stones heated, they re-radiated heat back to the fire, intensifying its temperature. Spaces between stones helped to funnel air to the fire in order to create optimum draft and higher combustion temperatures.

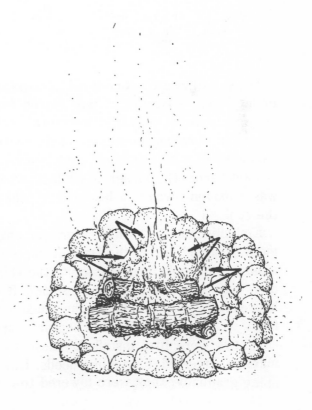

The stone firecircle served the human community well, even after it was moved from the open cave into the first structural enclosures. It remained, however, in its central location, affording an even distribution of radiant heat to the household while its smoke was removed through a hole at the peak of the roof.

Embellishments on this general arrangement occurred during the Dark Ages, when a louvered cupola, predecessor to the chimney, was built both to emit smoke from house interiors and to shelter the smoke hole from weather. In the 14th century, true chimneys were first installed. These were massive, inverted, funnel-like hoods. Developing gradually, they were lowered toward the firecircle, whose walls were extended upward. Eventually, these two elements were joined by decorative jambs on either side of the fire. Rudimentary at best, this became the fireplace as we know it today.

After these developments, the fireplace was next moved from its central site to a position against a wall. Since smoke emissions were now more controllable, it was possible to locate the fireplace anywhere in the dwelling, not necessarily in the center of the room directly under the smoke hole. Medieval builders also found that this alternative fireplace location made loft and second floor living space less encumbered. Even corner placement became common, especially in Scandinavian countries.

The fireplace mantle is a vestige of the early fireplace hood, which was relinquished as masons learned to support the chimney with side jambs and a back wall. By the 17th century, western European homes were being heated by a wood-burning fireplace with a deep firebox and a lofty, broad opening. Rising smoke carried most of the heat of the fire straight up, for there was no damper to control upward chimney draft. No grate maximized combustion, nor was there a smoke shelf to divert downdrafts.

The 17th century fireplace had a gluttonous appetite for fuel. However, wood and the labor for cutting it were abundant, so the economics of fireplace heating remained tolerable. Smokiness, however, was a universal annoyance plaguing every household, since cooking and water heating were also done at the open hearth.

About the middle of the 17th century, a schism took place among the proponents of wood-fueled heating. Seeing little future for the traditional, smoky, inefficient masonry fireplace of the day, one group turned to heating devices of metal, made possible by the newly acquired art of metal forging. By casting iron, it was found that proficient heating stoves could be mass-produced. Even today, in the growing circle of wood-heat enthusiasts, one still finds vocal advocates for the stove and equally vociferous champions of the fireplace.

From the time of this rupture to the present, the same arguments, pro and con, have persisted much as they did three hundred years ago. Efficiency statistics for stove-use appear indisputable, but the emotional argument for the esthetic appeal of the fireside is as persuasive now as then.

Fireplace devotees began working to ameliorate the problems of the 17th century fireplace. First and most notable among these was the Frenchman, Louis Savot. In 1620, Savot built an improved fireplace, which, if duplicated today, would be considered on a par with the most efficient, progressive designs now available. Indeed, the Savot fireplace contained heat-conserving features which are yet to be fully appreciated and implemented by many of today's fireplace builders. Savot's remedy for the smoky fireplace was to reduce the size of the firebox opening. He also devised a grate that allowed combustion air to flow between fire and coals. To extract even more room heat from wood, Savot devised a metal-clad air chamber below the hearth and at the back of the firebox. Entering by an inlet at the hearth, air was heated and rose through the chamber to enter the room from ducts mounted below the mantle. This was, of course, the direct predecessor to the hot air-circulating fireplace, as we now know it.

Fifty years elapsed before the next major improvement in fireplace design. Prince Rupert, an Englishman, installed several metal baffle plates at the back of the fireplace. Smoke traversed these baffles, upward, over, downward, and then upward again, until its final release to the chimney. Considerable heat was, thus, reclaimed from smoke before it finally entered the chimney flue. The primary baffle was hinged to open so that, when a fire was first started in a cold chimney, smoke would bypass this labyrinth of routing. When sufficiently warmed, the hinged baffle was closed and the heated chimney drew smoke through the heat-absorbing passages at the back of the firebox. This was the first successful use of the descending flue. A hundred years later, Ben Franklin copied both Rupert's descending flue and Savot's heat-circulating jacket for his Pennsylvania Fireplace. Admittedly parsimonious by nature, Franklin belonged more among the advocates of stove heating than to the supporters of fireplace use, as seen in the fact that the Franklin stove was originally meant to be retrofitted into a fireplace.

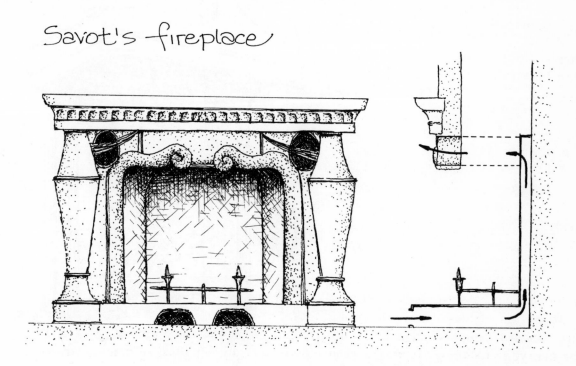

Savot's fireplace

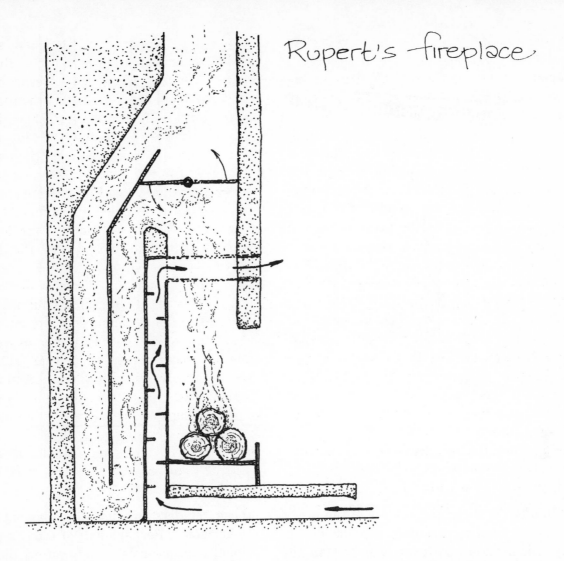

In the early 18th century, an American-turned-Englishman by the name of Count Rumford figured prominently in fireplace re-design. He was successful in alleviating the smokiness of the fireplace, for he designed and built a signally efficient unit. In the on-going wrangle over the virtues of the metal stove versus the open fireplace, Rumford took the position of fireplace purist, refusing to use metal part anywhere in his designs. "Metals of all kinds, which are well known to grow very hot when exposed to the rays projected by burning fuels," Rumford said, "are reckoned among the very worst materials that it is possible to employ in the construction of fireplaces." He brought the fire forward from seclusion in its deep box for everyone to enjoy. It was a rash move

reducing the size of the firebox, customarily 30 inches deep, to only 13 inches deep. Today, building codes restrict a builder to a firebox depth of no less than 20 inches.

Rumford inadvertently created the first smoke shelf by reducing the depth of the firebox, and limiting the throat opening to a mere 4-inch slot, as can be seen in the accompanying drawing. The narrow shelf created by this constriction arrests the downward movement of smoke into the room. A few years later, Franklin fitted a moveable metal plate into Rumford's restrictive throat opening, providing fireplace users with the first fireplace damper. To this day, commercially-sold throat dampers have about the same opening area as that specified by Rumford so many years ago.

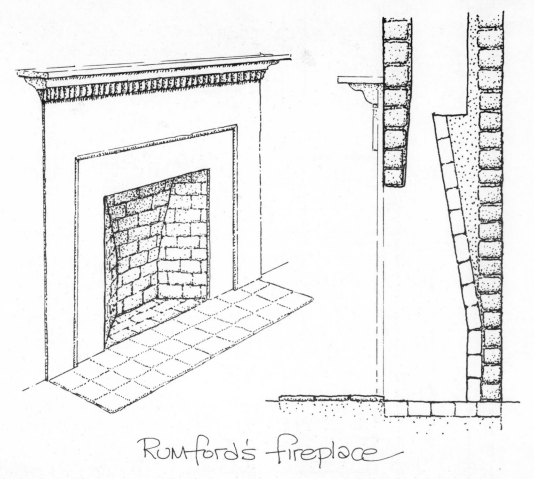

Rumford's Fireplace

Rumford was certainly aware of the many hot-air circulating fireplace designs of his day. His position, however, was that an all-masonry fireplace could provide more heat by radiance than could be gained through convected hot air. His fireplace maintained its high temperatures by absorbing and storing heat in a masonry lining of refractory material, like fireclay.

Next, Rumford determined that the best method for distributing heat about a room was by direct reflection from firebox walls, so he set about to increase this area of reflectivity. The side walls of the Rumford firebox were splayed to an exaggerated angle and the height of the firebox opening was increased to add to the area of effective radiation.

Fireplace builders tend to form a preference for that heating system which works best for themselves and their families, and these builders are usually adamant about their choice. Perhaps half of today's professional masons insist, as Rumford did, that only an all-masonry fireplace is an efficient one. Oddly enough, few of these contemporary masons have assimilated Rumford's innovative designs into their work. Apparently, his tall shallow fireplace has been forgotten over the years, while in its stead, deep squatty ones are most often found in modern homes.

The other half of today's fireplace builders are prejudiced in behalf of the hot-air circulating system. Unfortunately, they limit themselves to the use of cheaply-made manufactured units. In this book, we will offer improved designs for these systems and our own water-circulating one, so that readers may choose that method of fireplace heating which best suits their personal bias.

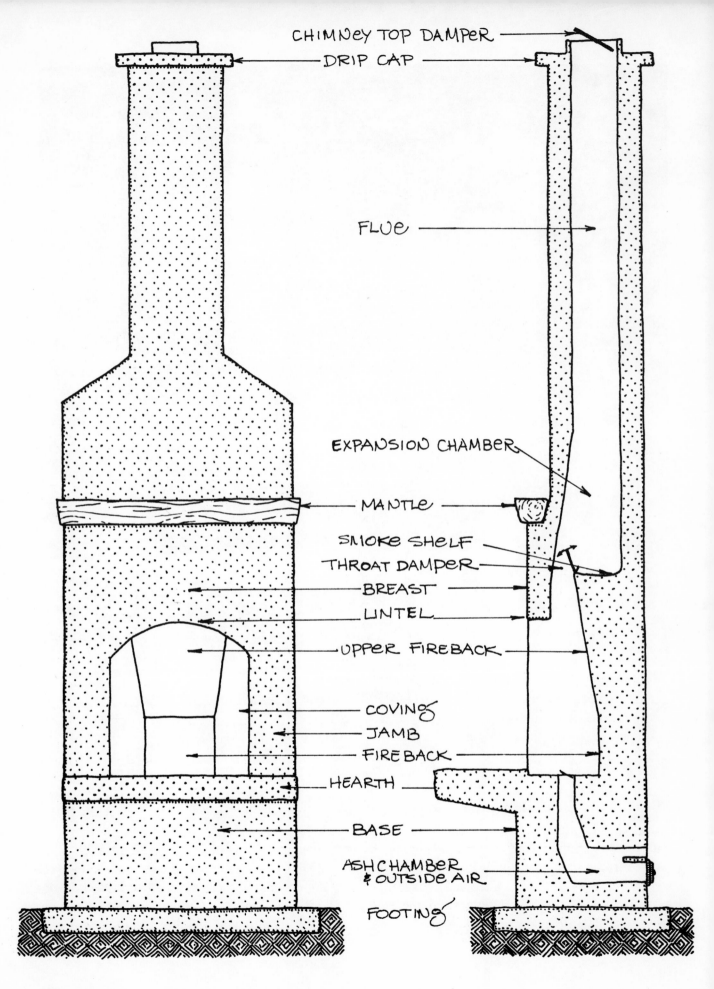

CHIMNEY TOP DAMPER

DRIP CAP

FLUE

EXPANSION CHAMBER

MANTLE

SMOKE SHELF

THROAT DAMPER

BREAST

LINTEL

UPPER FIREBACK

COVING

JAMB

FIREBACK

HEARTH

BASE

ASH CHAMBER & OUTSIDE AIR

FOOTING

18

The Chimney Effect

Many people have the notion that the master fireplace builder ranks with sorcerers and alchemists by having an ability to control the forces of nature. Admittedly, masons do little to dispel this image of themselves. Stories continue to circulate about the hiring of an eccentric mason, whose idiosyncracies are tolerated for fear that the fireplace owner will be cursed with a smoky chimney. It seems a shame to discourage such lore, but, in truth, anyone can build a working fireplace without a mystical awareness. Fireplaces draw only because hot air rises.

In actuality, it is the flue, not the firebox, that creates fireplace draft. A flue is an exceedingly simple structure. Opening inside the house, it is a vertical tube running from the firebox at its lower end to its opening on the outside of the house at its upper end. Before a fire is started, air both inside and outside the flue is approximately the same temperature and density. However, once a fire is lit in the firebox, combustion gases and smoke become heated, less dense, and start to rise up the chimney. Cooler air from the room rushes into the firebox to replace heated

air moving up the chimney, and in the process, it gives rising gases an additional upward push.

Once this surge is set in motion, it reinforces itself. As room air rushes into the firebox, it fans the fire, making it burn more rapidly and creating a stronger chimney current while still more air is drawn into the firebox. The factors which limit the indefinite increase of this process are the size of the fireplace opening, the capacity of the flue and, of course, the fuel supply.

A flue of given size can handle only a certain amount of moving air before the air begins to back up, just as excess water backs up in a drain pipe. Too the speed at which smoke-laden air may travel upward is limited by drag (or friction) against the walls of the flue. It is, therefore, possible for the fireplace to clog, spewing smoke back into the room. If the size of the fireplace opening is large, it allows more air to enter the firebox than the chimney can handle. Thus, the relationship between the size of the fireplace opening and the capacity of the flue is crucial to fireplace functioning.

Cross-sectional area is not the only factor determining flue capacity. Smoke travels up the flue in a spiraling motion. The more a flue pipe accomodates the spiraling path, the more efficiently it functions. A circular pipe is the optimal shape for a chimney flue, since it offers smoke its least impedance in its upward motion. Square and rectangular flues are more often used than round ones, simply because they adapt to a variety of building designs. But flues with these shapes require a larger cross-sectional area to accomodate the same amount of fumes that will rise in a circular flue.

The other important way to realize flue efficiency is to reduce the drag on flue walls. The inside of flue walls should be smooth so that smoke may spiral easily from bottom to top. Rough mortar joints,

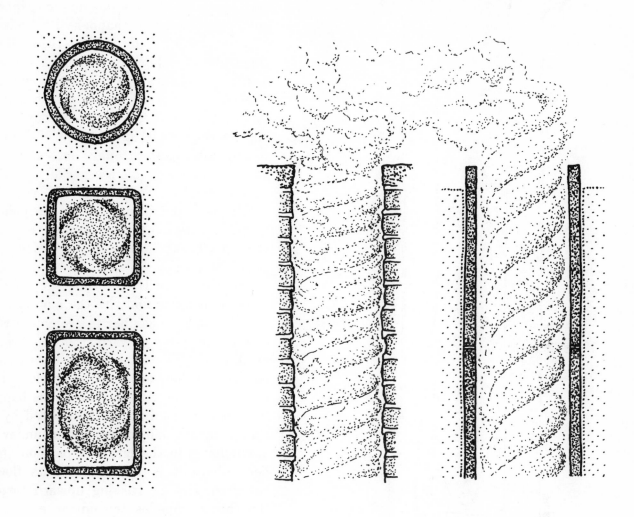

squared corners, and sudden chimney bends will cause eddying and flue wall resistance to smoke flow.

The height of the flue also affects draft. As a general rule, the taller a chimney, the better its draft. The reason for this is that a tall chimney contains a higher column of less dense hot air than a short one. Consequently, the total pull up the chimney is greater. On the other hand, this effect is counteracted if the chimney is so tall that flue gases are appreciably cooled as they rise, weakening the net draw. An overly large flue will also cause gases to cool. In this instance, the large cross-section area causes smoke to flow more slowly and thus to cool before it can escape.

The cooling of hot gases can be minimized by insulating flue walls from the rest of the chimney masonry. Once heated, these walls will not dissipate their heat to the masonry mass. As the fire burns low and ceases to promote a strong draft, hot flue walls will continue to draw smoke upward.

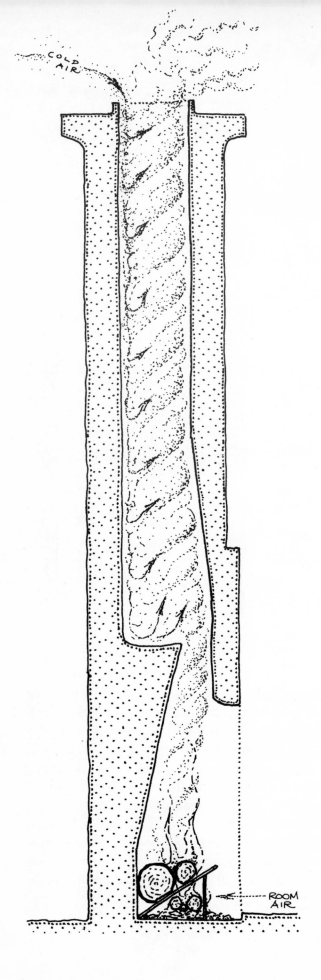

Since the chimney is open at both ends, it is as susceptible to cold air rushing down it as it is to hot air flowing up. If the flue is not operating to its maximum capacity, both phenomena can happen simultaneously. Generally, before they can deeply penetrate the chimney and even the firebox, cold downdrafts are warmed and their direction is reversed by escaping hot air. If this cold air does reach the firebox, it can impede the natural upward flow of the fire's smoke, causing it to billow into the room. This becomes a problem especially for short chimneystacks. The expansion chamber, smokeshelf, and throat, all at the point of transition between the firebox and flue, are specifically designed to reduce this possibility.

The throat, with its thin slit opening, works in conjunction with the more voluminous expansion chamber to promote a rapid flow of hot gases upward from the firebox, much as the Venturi principle increases lift on an air foil or carburetor flow in a gasoline engine. At the time this is happening, cold air from above is arrested by the throat in its fall down the chimney. It accumulates in the larger expansion chamber, where it is warmed and its flow is reversed. Hot air rushing upward through the throat impedes the entrance of these downdrafts into the firebox. It has been determined that the cross-sectional area of the throat must be approximately equal to the cross-sectional area of the flue. The placement of the throat should be toward the front of the firebox, considerably above the breast. Thus, smoke will not be able to find its way into the room.

Ironically, the same principle that causes the chimney to function well is also the force that must be overcome to maintain the heat efficiency of the firebox. If the chimney flue draws too well, the effect will be counter-productive. A large firebox opening and flue can easily draw more heated room air than they contribute in radiant heat to the house. Therefore, we do not recommend that fireplace openings be larger than 42 inches in width. Beyond this opening width, a fireplace gives diminishing returns unless an inordinate amount of wood is wastefully burned to rectify heat losses. Even a smaller fireplace can drain much warmth from the household if its fires are not carefully tended. The remainder of this book will concern itself with fireplace designs that remove the fire's smoke effectively, while retaining its heat.

As can be seen, there are many variables that affect the functioning of a fireplace. The danger exits with theoretical explanations that the novitiate will not know where to compromise the ideal for the sake of practicality. The purpose of the foregoing discussion has been to allow fireplace builders to think for themselves when designing their fireplaces, to minimize their rote dependance on prescriptive principles and proportions. Keep in mind that fireplace design need not be ideal to function. Many fireplaces draw acceptably, even when they are built with wide throats and uninsulated, rectangular flues. It is important to balance theory with the realities of the individual building project. If this were not often done, there would be few fireplaces in existence.

Since the principles of fireplace operation are so elementary, one may wonder at the absurdity that pervades the commonly held notion that masons wield magical powers in their influence on fireplace construction. For some healthy contrast to dispel this persisting illusion, we often relate the tale of the fireplace builder who constructed chimneys that mysteriously would not draw — until the work had been paid for. After payment, a brick was dropped down the flue, breaking a formerly invisible pane of glass that had blocked the passage.

Building Materials

No matter what you build, a better job will be done if you understand the properties of the building materials you use. Knowing what can and cannot be done with a given material, knowing its limits as well as its capabilities, will insure a structure that is stable and lasting. Building materials inappropriately used can cause disaster. The properties of fireplace building materials especially need to be known, for they undergo extraordinary changes in temperature and attack from moisture and smoke. Each building material must, therefore, be carefully selected to serve its function.

Too many fireplaces are built with little concern for their durability. It is often assumed that the fireplace is just another masonry project, and that the same mortar and stone which would make a strong, durable retaining wall would be appropriate for fireplace construction. The error of this assumption is often discovered when you examine the remains of an old stone fireplace. You will perhaps find that long ago it began to fall apart because the stone in its firebox could not withstand the heat of fires once made there. This may also be true of a more recently built fireplace whose firebrick are already falling out because they were laid with the wrong type of mortar. A well built fireplace should require little maintenance, few repairs, and last a lifetime. Our practical discussion of fireplace construction begins with a study of the component materials, hoping once the reader understands their qualities that they will be used as they should.

Stone

There is nothing quite like a stone fireplace. True, the aesthetic joys of watching fire flicker across rough stone cannot be disputed but if you want a lasting structure, confine your use of stone to those areas that do not get too hot. Most stone cannot withstand intense heat; in a firebox it soon fragments.

Stone covering a metal firebox.

The problem with using stone lies in the inconsistency of its makeup. It is common to be warned that rock surrounding a campfire may explode. Apparently, water trapped in stone crevices will reach the boiling point and trapped steam, under pressure causes the rock to explode. We authors have never heard of an entire stone fireplace exploding, but individual stones can and sometimes do burst. Used in a firebox, stone surfaces surely will spall and flake. This occurs because the face of stone heats faster than its interior, causing rapid surface expansion and consequent cracking. When stone, like granite, is not homogeneous it is particularly susceptible to destruction, for its various minerals expand at different rates.

Soapstone is the only natural mineral deposit suitable to withstand the intense heat and the rapid temperature change in a firebox. Although uncommon today, several hundred years ago it was not unusual to construct a firebox with five soapstone slabs: a floor, two covings, and two pieces comprising the fireback. Stone may be used in fireplace building, but its use should be limited to areas that do not receive direct exposure to heat. It should never be used to line the interior of a fireplace or chimney, although there is nothing dangerous about using stone on exterior surfaces. A properly built "stone" fireplace is therefore made of a ceramic or metal core surrounded by a shell of stone.

Ceramics

Of all the materials selected for use in the highly changeable conditions of the fireplace and chimney, ceramic products are doubtless the most useful and durable. Indeed, it is desirable to line fireplace interiors from firebox floor to chimney cap with ceramic products. The most commonly used ceramic materials are red brick, flue liners, and firebrick. To understand why they work well, consider how they are made.

The raw material of all ceramics is clay. Clay is a unique substance which is plastic and can be molded when taken from the earth in its moist state. But when fired at high temperatures, it becomes permanently hard and strong. There are many types of clay, each achieving individuality from the presence of various minerals in it, but all clay is chiefly composed of compounds of water, alumina, and silica. These are minute plate-like crystals which slide against one another on a film of water, giving this substance its plastic quality.

Clay is dug from the earth and refined of its rock and other impurities. In a moist state, it is molded to a desired shape and allowed to air dry. During this period, the watery film between the particles evaporates, leaving the clay intact and leathery. It can only be fired when dry, for moisture will expand and crack clay in the kiln.

During firing, clay is heated to temperatures of 1000-2000 degrees Farenheit. Its alumina-silica compounds melt and break down, then regroup into new crystals and a type of glass that permeates and bonds the whole crystalline structure. The hotter the firing, the more tiny pores between the clay crystals are filled, making the structure stonger and more dense. This process is called vitrification. Manufacturers of ceramic products must decide how hard and dense—

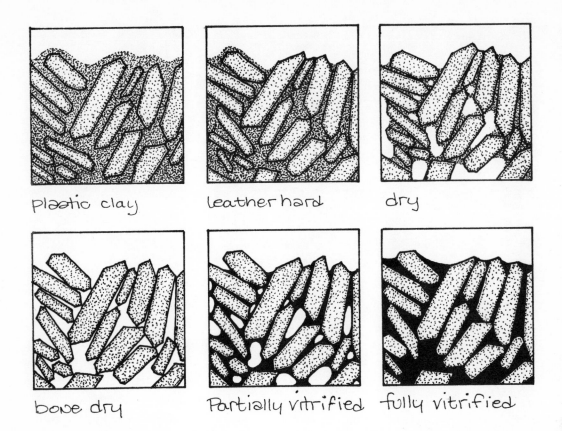

plastic clay   leather hard   dry

bone dry   Partially vitrified   fully vitrified

that is, how vitrified—they want them to be. For instance, it is desirable for bricks to be somewhat porous so that they can be split without shattering and can bond better with mortar.

Of course, different clays have different properties after firing. The clay used for making most brick and terra cotta flue liners is called shale. Its red color comes from its iron content. Shale fires to an extremly hard and durable building material that will resist moisture and chemical deterioration. Born of high temperature, it can withstand heat better than most other fireplace building materials, including metal and concrete. There are, however, other types of clay that are better for fireplace construction.

For hundreds of years, red clay brick was considered the best possible material with which to line a fireplace and chimney. Unlike metal, red brick does not deteriorate with moisture, nor do chemicals from soot and smoke affect it. These bricks withstand the high temperatures of fire for many years,

but eventually they spall and crack, particularly in those areas subject to the most extreme temperature change. Thermal shock is a major problem for fireplace building materials. It is not temperature intensity that cannot be withstood but the rapid heating and cooling occurring in the fireplace throughout its lifetime. Temperature fluctuations weaken brick, which expand, contract and eventually deteriorate. Furthermore, the surface of brick heats more than its interior, causing surface crumbling and internal stress and possible cracking.

Although they are above the hottest area of the fireplace, terra cotta flue liners also are subject to thermal cracking, not because of temperature intensities but because of rapid temperature shifts. We are not recommending that red clay materials be avoided in fireplace construction but that their limits be acknowledged. For instance, terra cotta liners should always be backed with solid masonry.

In the firebox where the highest heat is

Detail showing the particulate structure of firebrick.

generated, it is best to use firebrick, a special brick developed to withstand temperature extremes and variations. Firebricks are generally buff colored and larger than red brick. They are made from fireclay of which there are many varieties, among which are kaolineite, bauxite, and pyraphilite. All of these fireclays have one quality in common; they contain a much higher percentage of alumina than other clays. This substance gives clay a higher melting point and a smaller coefficient of expansion. These qualities make fireclay products less susceptible to the thermal shock mentioned above.

Fireclay brick is made by a different process than that used to make red clay brick. Firebricks are composed of a mixture of prefired clay particles and unfired clay. The size of the fired particles and their proportion to unfired clay determine the brick's rate of shrinkage and its resistance to thermal shock. To achieve uniformity of size and shape, firebrick is made more carefully than red brick. This special care makes fireclay products more expensive but also more durable than other ceramic products. They

should be used where there is intense heat. When buying firebrick, be careful to select a product of good quality, for many building suppliers will sell poor quality buff brick with which to line fireboxes. Although these brick look like firebrick and are made from kaoline clay, they do not go through the manufacturing process mentioned above and will not perform satisfactorily over the years.

Ceramic products are not adaptable to every aspect of fireplace building. In addition to strength and heat resistance, other qualities need to be considered. For instance, clay is not a rapid conductor of heat, although it does absorb heat slowly and will retain it for a long period of time. When designing your fireplace, use ceramic products to retain heat but avoid them when you wish to release heat rapidly, as in heat exchangers. Because they do not absorb heat rapidly, bricks are a good material to reflect the heat of the fire into a room. Because it releases heat slowly, a ceramic-lined fireplace will continue to radiate heat a long time after the fire is extinguished.

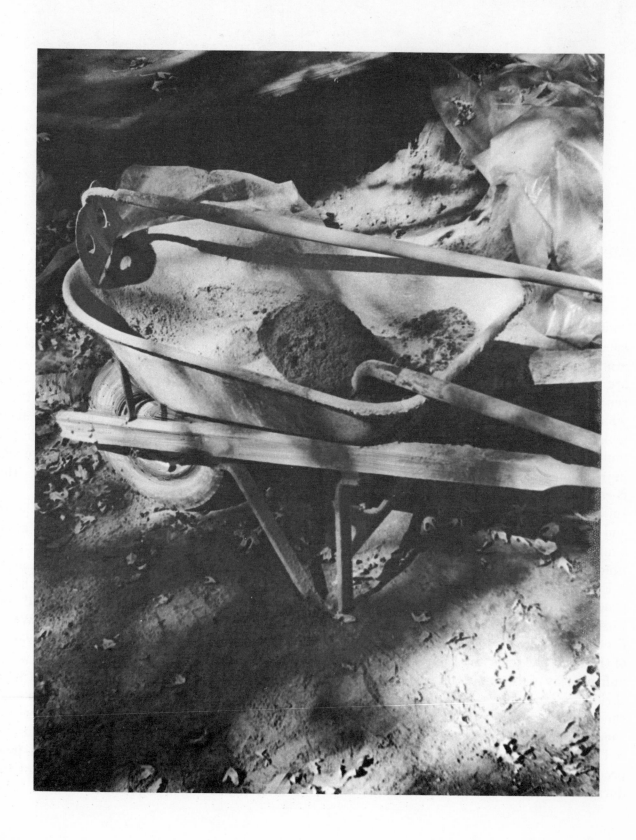

The basic constituent of poured concrete, building block, and most of the mortars used in masonry work is Portland cement. When mixed with aggregate and water, it sets to stone-like hardness and has high compressive strength and resistance to environmental deterioration.

A mixture of lime, gypsum, and clay, with traces of silica, alumina, and iron, primarily constitute Portland cement. These components are mixed, ground together, and then burnt in a kiln at temperatures of around 2700 degrees Farenheit. The clinker thus formed is pulverized into a fine powder, which passes through a sieve with 40,000 openings per square inch. When this powder is mixed with water, a chemical reaction takes place, forming a new compound that hardens permanently. Since water is required in the reaction it is called a hydraulic cement.

When Portland cement combines with aggregate and water, it bonds the particles together, giving body and strength to the mixture. Small aggregate, like sand, makes mortar. The addition of gravel makes concrete. Adding hydrated lime makes a plastic, workable mortar suitable for brick laying.

Because it is hydraulic, Portland cement should be kept moist while it is hardening or

curing. Its hardening continues for years. In a warm moist environment, however, concrete will reach most of its strength in a month's time. The primary deterrents to the curing process are freezing temperatures and dry heat. Freezing temperatures arrest hydration by turning water to ice, which expands and causes concrete to disintegrate. Dry heat, on the other hand, evaporates water from the mix, causing an incomplete reaction. The fireplace builder must be particularly wary of the latter, for using a fireplace too soon after its erection may cause weak and powdery mortar. A month should be the minimum waiting period between final construction and first use. A better practice would be to build in the spring so there will be a whole summer for proper curing.

If correctly mixed and water cured, Portland cement concrete, building block, and mortar will withstand fireplace heat almost as well as red brick. Again, it is not the intensity of heat but the rapid change in temperature that causes structural deterioration. On the fireplace exterior where the temperature range is narrow and variations occur slowly, concrete, block, and mortar should last indefinitely. In the firebox, however, mortar and concrete will quickly crack due to rapid expansion and contraction, eventually crumbling to dust. Portland cement mortar has a melting point of just 1400 degrees Farenheit and may actually melt in the hottest parts of the firebox. Here, only refractory bricks and special heat resistant mortars should be used.

In the chimney flue and expansion chamber, judgement must be exercised in the use of Portland cement materials. In most fireplace designs, Portland cement mortar holds up tolerably well. Although it may crack, mortar will not crumble if properly cured. Mortar joints between bricks and flue liners should be thin, as a general rule. Some chimney designs, however, divert smoke downward and carry it upward through circuitous routes, causing intense heat build-up in the area of the flue. It is to its designer's credit that a chimney can maintain such high temperatures, but this necessitates building with refractory materials instead of Portland cement mortar. It is best to take the most cautious approach in these special constructions, for the initial investment in the proper materials will make future repair less necessary and therefore less expensive.

Concrete and Mortar Proportions

Concrete for footings—
1 portland cement: 3 sand: 4 gravel.

Concrete for floors and cantelevered hearths—
1 portland cement: 2 sand: 3 gravel.

Mortar for laying stone—
1 portland cement: 3 sand or
1 portland cement: 1/2 hydrated lime: 4 1/2 sand or
1 mortar mix: 3 sand.

Mortar for brick and block laying—
1 portland cement: 1 hydrated lime: 6 sand or
1 mortar mix: 3 sand.

Mortar for parging and stuccoing—
1 portland cement: 1 hydrated lime: 4 sand or
1 mortar mix: 2 sand.

Refractory Cement

The use of high temperature cement products is, unfortunately, not well known to most masons. It is commonly thought that the home fireplace cannot generate temperatures requiring the use of specialized refractory materials. This is a misconception, however, and as highly efficient fireplaces that do kindle high temperatures become increasingly popular, the need for familiarity with this line of products becomes a compelling matter. The variety of choices for specialized refractory cements is surprising, while bewildering. There are dry and wet mixes, heat- and air-setting types, mortars for various heat ranges, malleable materials much like modeling clay that can be pounded into place, and heat resistant concretes that can be cast. The awareness that such materials exist makes it possible to create innovative fireplaces which will accomodate high temperatures.

Fireclay is the basic constituent of most refractory mortars, as it is of firebrick. A mixture of fired and unfired clay particles is combined with water to form a mortar used for laying firebrick in high temperature kilns. When used for this purpose, the mortar is allowed to dry thoroughly, but not until its first firing does it become fixed. At this time, it develops a ceramic bond with the firebricks of the kiln. This is called **heat-setting** mortar.

Unlike a kiln, a firebox is not entirely suited to heat-setting mortars. Although

Burned out mortar.

36

the area near the fire gets hot enough to create ceramic bonding, the more remote areas never reach a temperature sufficient to set mortar. To build a firebox you, therefore, need another type of refractory cement, one with **air-setting** quality. This need is met by mixing fireclay with sodium silicate. Commonly called water glass, sodium silicate contains the elements of ordinary glass but is soluble in water. However, once exposed to air, the water evaporates and the silica reorganizes into a hard, glassy gel. When combined with fireclay to form mortar, the mix will set at room temperature. At high temperatures, this fireclay mixture still forms a ceramic bond. Such air-setting mortars are, therefore, ideally suited for fireplace building. They are available in a dry form, but we recommend the wet mix. It comes in cans, combined with the correct amount of water.

Although it is not needed for ordinary fireplace construction, a refractory concrete with a Portland cement base is also available. The Portland cement is given greater heat resistance by raising its alumina content. This mixture would be useful for forming thin, concrete fireplace hoods or for casting component parts for fireplace interiors. One can also find refractory insulating cements for areas of the fireplace in which it is desirable to retain heat, such as around flue liners.

Most masonry supply outlets do not carry the materials mentioned here. If they do stock fireclay mortar, it may be the wrong type for fireplace construction. Investigate before purchase. A more likely source would be a company that builds and repairs boilers and kilns, or you may have to order directly from a manufacturer. An additional drawback is the expense of refractory materials, for which one can expect to pay twice as much as for their nonrefractory counterparts. These products should be used with discretion, but where necessary, they are indispensable.

Metal parts undergo considerable stress in fireplaces. Generally, they are more vulnerable to deterioration and to deformation than fireplace masonry. They are often the first components to need attention. Fireplace masonry should last, say, a hundred years with little maintenance, but metal parts often need repair in ten years or less. Metals commonly used in fireplace construction are found in the ferrous category of elements — those derived from iron. Except for the occasional use of copper for hoods, ferrous metals are best suited for use in fireplaces because of their workability and relative cheapness. We will now consider the properties of ferrous metals which make them useful yet not entirely trouble-free in fireplace construction.

Although, as will be shown later, various deritivities of iron have their individual properties, all ferrous metals are vulnerable to some degree of corrosion. This fact must be considered when designing the metal parts of a fireplace. Corrosion is the deterioration of metal through its combination with various elements of the atmosphere. The most common form of corrosion is oxidation, the slow burning up of metal as it combines with oxygen. The residue formed in this process is iron oxide or rust, that reddish substance which flakes from metal surfaces. Oxygen and water must be present for metal to rust, and heat will accelerate the process. The fireplace is, therefore, an ideal environment for forming rust on metal components. Flue dampers often sit in rain water, and combustion gases also contain water which causes rust to form. Iron oxides also form when metal is heated to a cherry red glow. This is why grates "burn out" and why flakes of metal scale from the lower backs of metal fireboxes.

There are other forms of corrosion. Ferrous metals can be attacked by any number of acids which react to form destructive compounds. Carbon dioxide dissolved in rain forms carbonic acid. Smoke contains sulfur dioxide which forms sulfuric acid when dissolved in water. Both of these acids deteriorate ferrous metals. Corrosion is a problem when using these metals, and although it cannot be prevented, various steps may be employed to minimize the effects. Protective paints will help to prevent surface corrosion, although it must be heat resistant or it will burn away, exposing the metal to corrosive deterioration. Another method used to protect metals from corrosion is to coat them with a thin layer of non-corrosive metal, such as zinc. This process is called galvanization. Metals thus treated, however, are not suitable for fireplace use, for the zinc will discharge poisonous fumes as it burns off.

Another problem with metal is its tendency to become distorted or to change shape when subjected to intense heat. Distortion can occur when metal fireplace parts are being cut with a torch during fabrication or when the finished metal has been installed and is in use. Examples can be found in the warped backs of heat forms or in damper doors which become curved and fail to properly seat. Metals also react to heat in another way; they expand and contract. Because they expand at a greater rate than adjoining masonry, the masonry may crack if precautions are not taken.

Various metals have differing properties which are the key to their usefulness. There are three main types of metal commonly used in fireplaces: cast iron, sheet and plate steel, and stainless steel.

Cast iron is shaped in a mold. It is a strong but brittle substance, which will break rather than bend. Although inflexi-

Fireplace with metal firebox, expansion chamber, flue, and removable door.

ble, it has the advantage of not being subject to warping when heated. It will, however, crack if it changes temperature too rapidly. Relatively resistant to corrosion, its surface may rust, but this oxidation will form a crust, preventing further penetration. Because of its resistance to distortion and corrosion, cast iron is desirable for use in fireplaces. However, its use is limited for most owner-builders, because it must be cast to a desired shape. This requires a process that is possible only with large scale manufacturing techniques. If you cannot find a needed cast iron part, you will have to fabricate one from sheet metal.

Sheet and plate steel are produced by rolling ingots of cast iron until they become a specified thickness. The only difference between the two is that plate metal is thicker and measured in fractions of an inch whereas the thinner sheet metal is meas-

ured in terms of its gauge. (During the rolling process, the molecular organization of the steel is changed so that it acquires different properties from those of cast iron. Sheet steel becomes more flexible and less brittle so that it can be bent to shape. It can also be welded to other pieces of metal. Unfortunately, sheet steel is more subject to corrosion and distortion than cast iron. When building fireplace parts that will contact intense heat, smoke, or water, it is wise to use a thickness of steel greater than that which is structurally required. Thicker metal is less subject to distortion and is more slowly corroded.

Even using the thickest plate steel, you should still design your system with the thought that someday the two most vulnerable areas in the fireplace will have to be repaired or replaced. These are the lower fireback, which comes in direct contact with

40

the fire, and the damper door, which receives abuse both from the heat and smoke of the fire and from water.

Sheet and plate steel is fabricated by the welding process, which is the fusion of two pieces of metal using intense heat. A welding rod if often used to strengthen and fill the connecting joint between the two pieces. A properly welded seam is known to be stronger than the original metal.

Another type of metal is stainless steel, a sheet metal which is more resistant to corrosion than ordinary mild steel. This is because it has a high chromium content, which makes the steel more dense, less porous, and less susceptible to corrosion. Parts made from stainless steel will last longer than those made from mild steel. Unfortunately, stainless steel is expensive and can only be cut and welded with special equipment. In most cases the advantage gained is not worth the cost. It can be recommended, however, for thin metal flue pipe and internal pieces not easily replaced, such as an inaccessible damper door.

Despite problems with using metals in fireplaces, their use is unavoidable. The relative strength and flexibility of metal compared to masonry make it irreplaceable for doors, dampers, and other moving parts. Its heat conducting properties make it desirable for heat recovering systems. When using metal, design for its limitations. If you anticipate the replacement of a metal part at some point within the lifespan of the masonry structure, install it so that it may be repaired or removed with as little hassel as possible.

The Sturges metal heat exchanger.

Glass

Increasingly, glass doors are being used in fireplace design. Glass doors have the advantage of being transparent, allowing you to view your fire while preventing room air from escaping up the chimney. It is also unique among building materials because of its internal structure. Primarily, it is composed of silica and small quantities of lime and soda. From their raw form, sand and limestone are melted together in a process using temperatures of around 1700 degrees Farenheit. Molten glass is formed and gradually cools; i.e., it anneals. This must take place slowly, for otherwise internal stress, created by differential hardening, will cause the glass to crack. Once cooled, it is rigid and brittle, but, strictly speaking, not solid. Since it does not crystallize, glass is considered to be a superviscous liquid.

Glass fireplace doors are subject to rapid temperature variations and rough treatment due to careless handling or popping wood. Both of these problems make regular window glass unsuitable for fireplace doors. There is no problem with over-heating for glass doors will never melt from mere fireplace heat. But there is a problem with rapid temperature change. When regular glass heats too quickly, it expands faster than it can hold together and it shatters. If the same glass is heated slowly it will remain intact. To resolve this problem, a type of glass was developed which contains boron oxide. With this addition, glass expands less readily and will not break during temperature fluctuations. The common name for this glass is pyrex. The strength of glass is determined by the strength of its surface. Therefore, tempered glass was developed for use. Regular glass is reheated to just below its softening point and is then suddenly cooled by subjecting both of its surfaces to jets of air. This causes the outside surface, which cools faster, to be in a state of compression, while the inner portion is in a state of tension. The two stresses being in balance give the surface of glass its increased strength. However, for this reason, the slightest scratch or flaw in the surface of tempered glass will cause it to shatter.

Do not assume that glass transmits the entire electromagnetic spectrum merely because it is transparent to visible light. Glass inhibits passage of most of the heat or infrared rays of fire. The value of glass doors is, therefore, more esthetic than useful.

Wood

In former times, chimneys were built of logs and mud, but evidence of this can only be found written in history books. For obvious reasons, wood is not a good building material to contain fire. Fireplaces are, however, commonly surrounded by wood, and some builders allow wood structural members to bear directly on the fireplace. It is still necessary, therefore, to consider the hazards of building with wood in the proximity of fire.

The primary necessity is to establish a distance between wood and masonry safe enough to prevent fire danger. There is no simple rule to determine this; the best approach is to use common sense. Consider how it is possible for wood to ignite when it is built in contact with fireplace masonry.

Suppose a ceiling joist is built against the masonry of a chimney with six inch walls. The masonry rarely becomes hotter than 150 degrees Farenheit — even with prolonged use — and green wood must reach 700 degrees to ignite. The arrangement seems safe. However, over the years this wooden members dries and eventually becomes fire-ready. A chimney fire, heating the masonry surface to only 250 degrees, can then kindle this joist, once tars and combustible gaseous residues have accumulated on the surface. It is a slow but inevitable process and one which must be reckoned with when you want to build a safe dwelling.

Most codes demand a clearance of two inches between fireplace masonry and surrounding wood framework. In the example given above, this is a wholly reasonable requirement. Other areas of a fireplace more removed from the source of heat do not need such clearance.

Indeed, there need be nothing wrong with resting beams on the structure of the fireplace if proper precautions are taken. Such members must be remote from the source of heat, and if there is any doubt about the safety of their placement, they should be insulated or anchored apart from the masonry with joist hangers.

Knowledgeable commonsense remains the criterion for building with wood in proximity to fireplaces. Once in use, regular inspection of nearby wood will also assure fireplace safety.

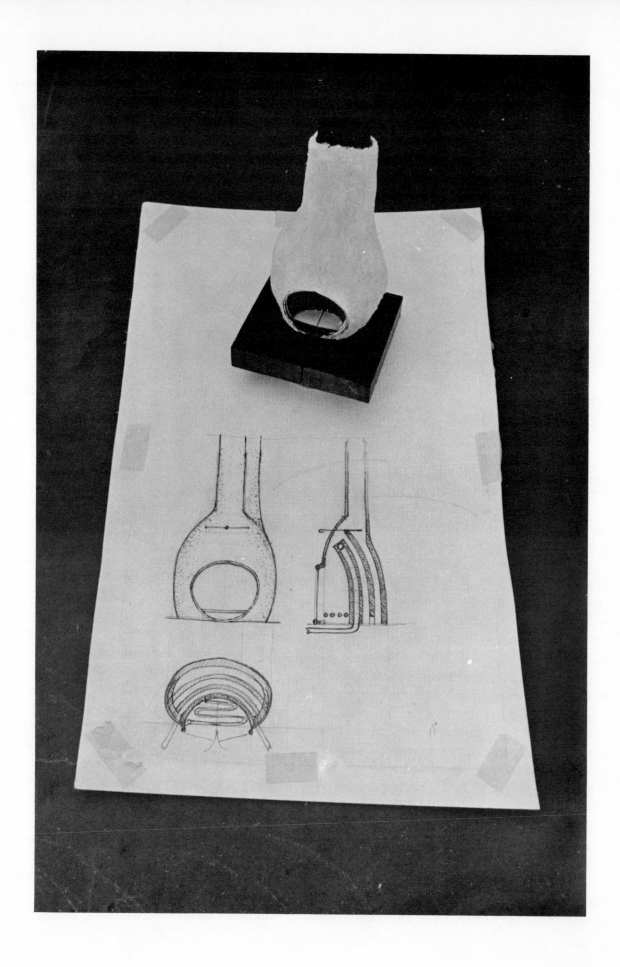

Preparation

Before the first brick may be laid, there is much preliminary work to be done when building a fireplace. A design must be selected, a work schedule set, and materials gathered. Although this aspect can be rather uninteresting compared to the actual work of fireplace construction, without proper preparation there will inevitably be problems and hold-ups later in the job. A fireplace is a complex structure, made of numerous design factors and materials. And to the extent that it passes through floor, ceiling, and roof, a fireplace is integral to the design of the house.

The Plans

A fireplace is difficult to visualize for those who have never built one. It is basically a hollow, vertical structure, with varying space requirements at every height of its construction. This difficulty is increased if a complex design is planned, one including air vents, several fireboxes, and multiple flues. Plan ahead. Make sure that the lower part of the fireplace incorporates a large enough area to include the workings to be built above. Make detailed drawings to aid your visualization of the entire structure. These scale drawings should include a front and side elevation and a number of cross sections which view internal structural changes. For complicated designs, we recommend that you even build a scale model.

Special attention should be given to the placement of the ash dump, to firebox arrangement, to the area comprising the chimney throat and smoke shelf, to how several flues will fit the alloted chimney space, and to details of the wood framing which skirts the chimney. Scale drawings and a model are aids which may prevent the error of placing two parts in the same conflicting space. They help to determine what the outside dimensions of the fireplace should be.

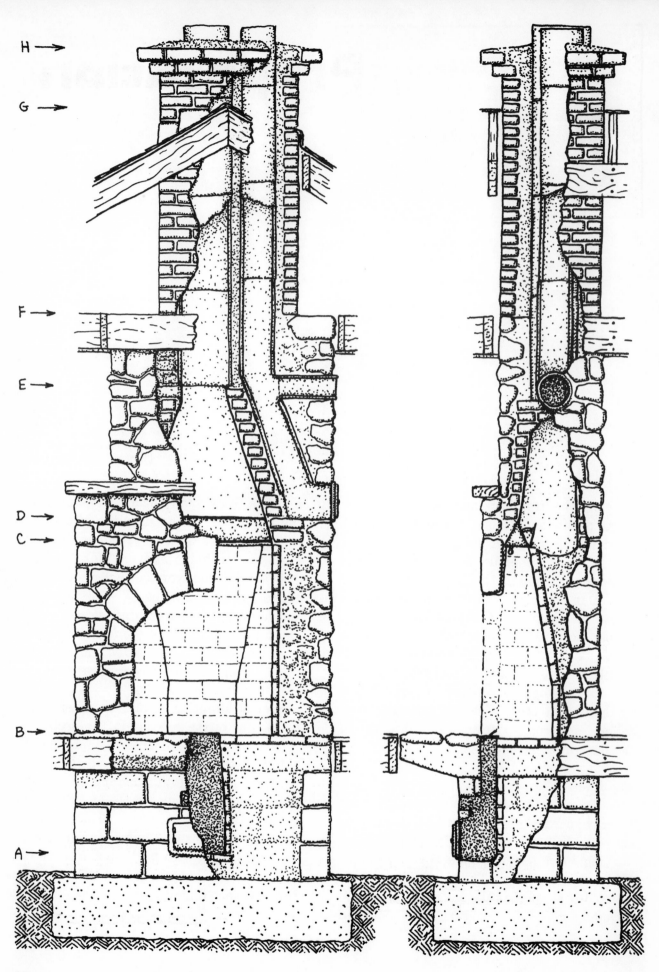

H →
G →
F →
E →
D →
C →
B →
A →

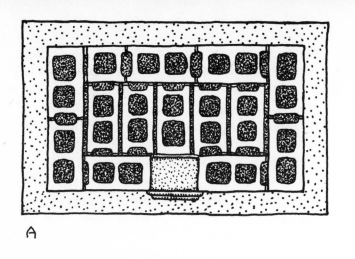

A

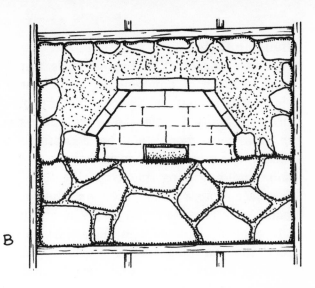

B

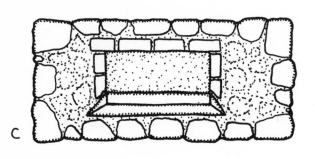

C

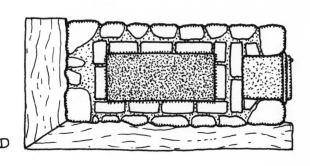

D

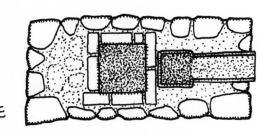

E

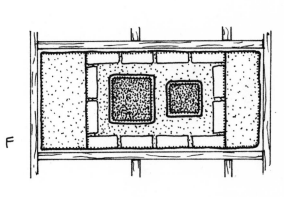

F

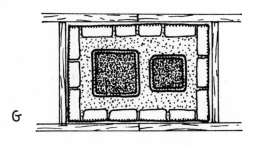

G

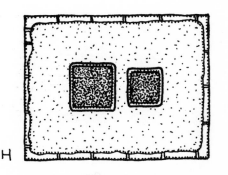

H

Building Codes

Before construction begins, it is important to learn of any building code restrictions which may apply to your fireplace project. Many fireplace designs suggested in this book would not be acceptable in many building code jurisdictions, while some building department specifications for fireplace construction are, on the other hand, not acceptable to us. We attribute this schism of purpose in large part to the fact that fireplace codes were originally written by tradition-bound, retired masons who were disinterested in innovative fire-place improvement. Keep this in mind when you confront the building department in your county with your chosen design. Be ready to explain in detail why your design is superior in every respect to the code approved model.

Not all code requirements for fireplace construction are, of course, unwarranted. The requirement for four 1/2-inch steel reinforcing bars set vertically from foundation to chimney and tied horizontally at 18-inch intervals with 1/4-inch steel ties is not unreasonable, for instance, in earthquake country. Anchoring the chimney at

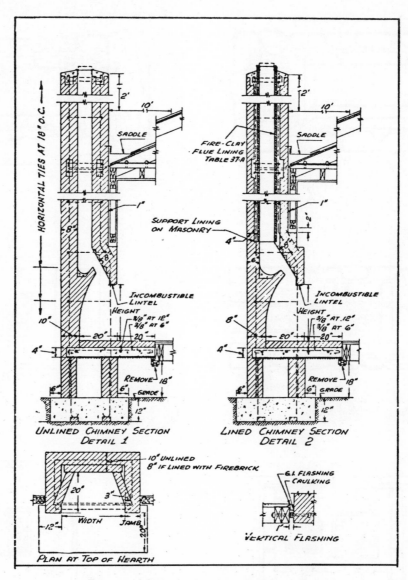

Excerpted from the Uniform Building Code

each floor or at ceiling level with two 1-inch steel straps is also a wise code requirement. These straps must also be embedded in 12 inches of chimney masonry.

We agree that some code stipulations do echo sensible masonry practice. The fireplace foundation does need to be a foot thick and should extend 6 inches beyond fireplace walls. It must, of course, be placed below frost level on undisturbed soil. Fireplace masonry facing should be no less than 8 inches thick, and joints between firebrick should not exceed a quarter of an inch.

You can, however, anticipate disapproval from the building department if you intend to use an owner-built air-circulating metal fireplace jacket. If they care to do so, building officials can demand a certificate of licensed welding for your fabricated heat jacket. They can also require approval of your design from the Fire Underwriters Board.

Like the conventional mason, the building inspector is often skeptical about the shallow depth and the tall opening of a Rumford-style fireplace. We await a test case of this issue to bring about the re-writing of this part of the building code. Meanwhile, unless they stick to the letter of the local building code, owner-builders can anticipate a certain amount of hassel from their country building department. It will be claimed that a Rumford-type of fireplace will create undue smoke annoyance or pose a fire hazard. If necessary, approach the Chief Building Inspector with your fireplace proposal or go directly to your County Board of Appeals. You can even argue that, after all, it is you who must supply wood fuel for your fireplace, that no subsidy will be forthcoming from City Hall for this purpose. The code is, from our point of view, negligent in its insistence that the public health can only

Vertical reinforcing in a fireplace base.

be served by a homeowner's use of heating facilities that are grossly inefficient and inappropriate.

Scheduling

Once the fireplace plan is completed, a materials list and a construction schedule can be made. Although it is not realistic to make a strict schedule, it is helpful to plan fireplace construction to complement house construction. For example, tight spaces in which brick must eventually be laid can be avoided. You can also plan rough framing so so that it will support masonry scaffoling and carry guide strings. On the other hand, you may find that you will not want to complete some of the framing until a certain portion of the fireplace is built in order for it to carry structural members. Such scheduling may well facilitate both masonry and

carpentry work.

Adding a fireplace to an existing structure requires different planning and scheduling. In this case, the fireplace must fit into pre-existing limitations. Once you have determined where you wish to place it, assess the possible problems of construction for each level. Ask yourself if there is a structural member that will have to be removed. Is there plumbing or wiring in the way? How will the chimney pass through the roof? How tall will the chimney have to be to reach safely above the roof? Will there be difficulty placing scaffolding on the roof? All these considerations must be made ahead of time or you may ultimately find yourself trying to build a fireplace around a bathtub!

Gathering Materials

Insofar as it is practical, all building materials should be at the site before construction begins. There are a number of reasons for this. If there is a question about

A Recommended Construction Schedule for Building a Fireplace

Pour footings and foundation and fireplace base at the same time.

Build masonry foundation walls and fireplace base at the same time.

The fireplace base should be built to the height of the bottom of the floor joist. To wait til later would necessitate crawling under the house.

Install floor joists and subfloor.

Box in for the fireplace and the hearth.

Frame and close in house.

Box in for the places where the chimney passes through the ceiling and roof but do not cut out these areas until necessary.

Complete construction of fireplace, hearth, and chimney.

Waiting until the house is closed in protects the masonry from the weather and allows work on rainy days.

The framing can be used to support scaffolding and guidelines.

Complete finish work on house

Because fireplace building is such a messy process, its best to let the finish work wait until the masonry construction is complete.

the size of any fireplace component, it should be on hand for immediate reference. If a piece is to be custom fabricated, defer preparation of a space for its installation until it is built. Handmade parts are often less true to specified dimensions than manufactured items. Brick, mortar, flue liners, and refractory materials should all be ordered in advance of construction, for often building suppliers will not stock the specialized materials you require, with delivery taking many additional weeks. Fireclay mortar and round flue liners generally require special ordering. If they are not available when needed, work will be delayed.

Acquiring Skills

Requisite building skills are as important to the job as the necessary materials. Mixing and finishing concrete, laying brick, and welding metal — all are necessary to the building of a fireplace. In following chapters, the basic tenants of some skills will be discussed. Acquisition of skills may also be learned from reading books on the subject or acquired through direct experience with tradesmen. Visiting building sites and taking extension courses can be helpful. We know of an owner-builder who welded a metal firebox and damper in an adult high school welding class, using scrap metal and

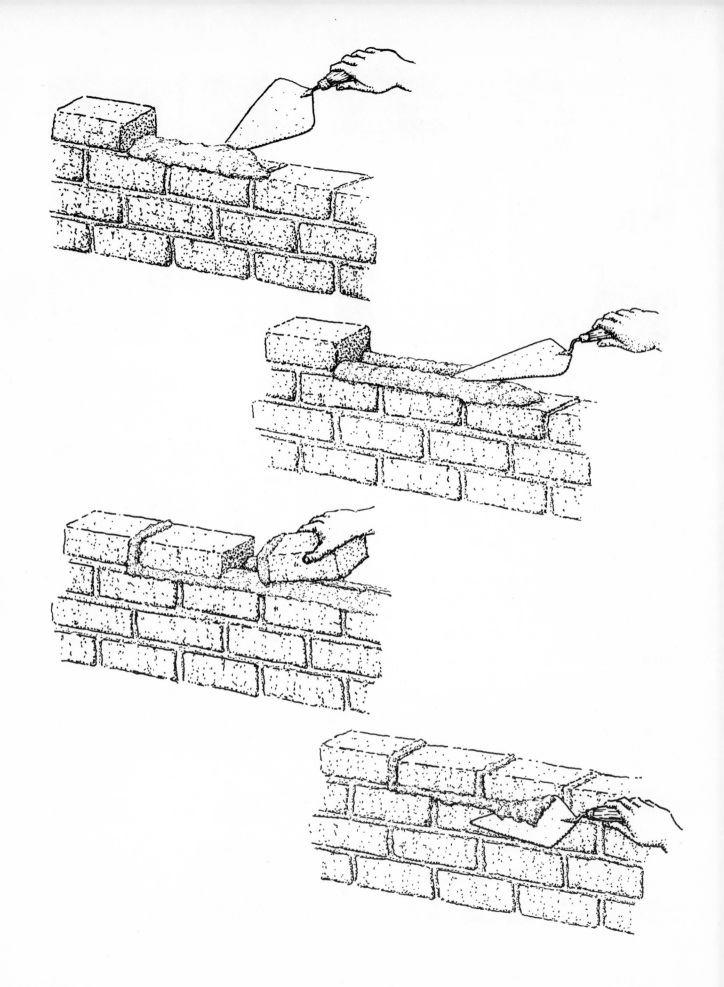

the school's equipment. Experience through direct participation is the only way to master a trade.

Masonry skills are especially intimidating to a beginner. Many owner-builders will do the carpentry, plumbing, and electrical work on their house but hire a mason to build their fireplace. Enough basic masonry, however, can easily be learned by the novitiate mason when sound instruction is received from reliable sources.

Tools

To accompany acquired skills, you will need a variety of quality tools. It is invariably easiest and fastest to use the tool designed for the job to be done. Tools of professional quality should be purchased rather than less expensive ones, which do not perform as well and quickly wear out. Even a tool as simple as a trowel can be poorly made. When selecting a trowel, examine the weld where handle and blade meet, observe the quality of its steel, and feel its weight and balance.

Chimney building requires masonry, concrete mixing, carpentry, and even metal working tools. For a full discussion of the use and kinds of masonry tools, see our book, **Stone Masonry**, $6, available from Owner-Builder Publications, P. O. Box 550, Oakhurst, CA 93644.

Fireplace Building

Actually, a fireplace has two intertwining structures. Generally, when people admire a fireplace they see only its outward structure, its facade. The shape, type of stone, mantle, and hearth comprise its outer shell; they are still only the surface characteristics of a fireplace. An experienced mason will also value these fireplace elements but not to the exclusion of an appreciation of the inner

Cutting a flue liner with a masonry saw blade.

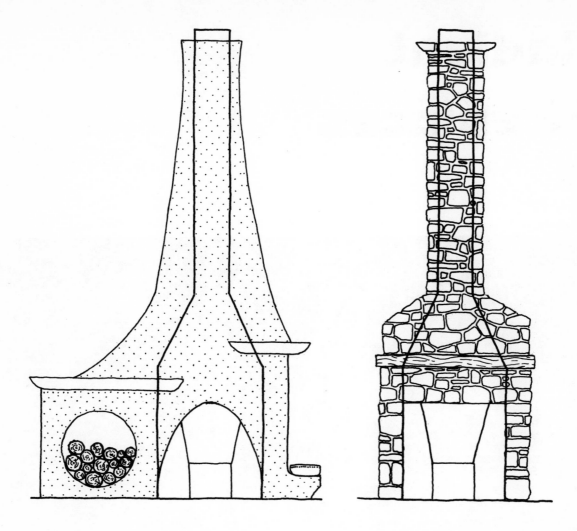

structure: the shape of the firebox, placement of the damper, and the size of flue liners. It is these latter factors that determine how well an attractive fireplace will draw smoke and how much radiant heat it will emit.

In following discussions of fireplace construction, we will emphasize the building of the inner structure. We consider the outer, visible aspect of the fireplace much like clothing, inasmuch as it serves to support, cover, and decorate the inner workings of the structure. Like clothing, fireplace apparel may fit loosely or closely and still function. There is wide latitude in which each individual builder may and should exercise personal taste in creating a fireplace facade.

However, the inner structure must be assembled according to rules and with a precise formula of proportions. It is in this respect that we intend to relate the greatest detail of fireplace building. After all, if a fireplace is improperly constructed and fails to draw well or to heat the household, of what practical value is its attractive shell? It is merely a huge expensive sculpture.

The following chapters will describe the construction of three basic types of fireplaces. The first of these is the simple and traditional design similar to that which Count Rumford used two hundred years ago. It remains unsurpassed for its ability to radiate heat. The second type offers a capacity for hot air circulation, and the third, a capacity for heating with hot water.

Radiant Fireplaces

A wood fire, like the sun, heats by radiation. For example, even on a cold day, you feel warmed when standing in the sun. Or sitting by a burning fire you are warmed, even before room air becomes a comfortable temperature. The reason for this phenomenon is that infrared waves, radiating from wood fire or sunlight, strike your body and warm you directly. They do not so much heat the air around you as the surfaces of objects in that air space.

The primary source of heat from the fireplace is radiation from the burning fire. A well built fireplace is, therefore, one designed to convey a maximum amount of heat from radiant energy into the living space. Count Rumford understood this principle, and the firebox he designed leaves little need for improvement. The Rumford firebox was purposely shallow in order to reflect as much heat as possible into the room. Its opening exposed the full height of a tall, slanted back and angled covings, which absorbed radiant heat from the fire and then reflected it roomward.

Rumford enunciated a set of standard proportions for his fireplace design. He specified that its opening be as high as it was wide, its depth be a third of its opening width, and its back wall be the same dimension as its depth. We have built, used, and varied these firebox proportions and have arrived at a modified firebox design, illustrated herein, which can be practicably built with materials available today. The shape of the box has been altered to accomodate more wood for a longer burning fire, without — we feel — sacrificing its capacity to efficiently provide quantities of radiant heat.

Consider the dimensions we prefer as merely suggestions, not as regulations. No single set of fireplace proportions is unalterable; they may be changed to adapt to your personal needs and preferences. Provided it remains structurally within certain limitations, the fireplace should function properly when completed. Remembering this, note that the area of the flue opening should be about one-tenth the area of the fireplace opening. The throat must be positioned toward the front of the firebox, at least eight inches above the lintel, its cross sectional area should be equal to that of the flue. A smoke shelf no less than 10 inches deep should be provided, and there must be no sharp directional changes in the expansion chamber or flue.

In this chapter, we have drawn in detail the construction sequence for a simple masonry fireplace and chimney. The accompanying photos illustrate this type of fireplace, picturing one that was added to the outside of an existing house. Construction techniques for this fireplace are equally applicable for a fireplace to be built entirely within a house. This simple design is the basis for many of the more complex fireplace designs offered elsewhere in this book, for we feel that the primary function of any fireplace is to radiate and reflect as much heat as possible into the living zone.

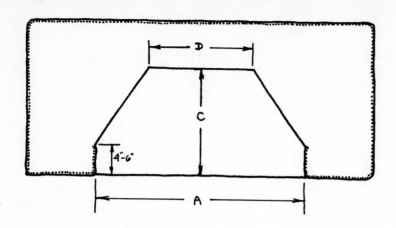

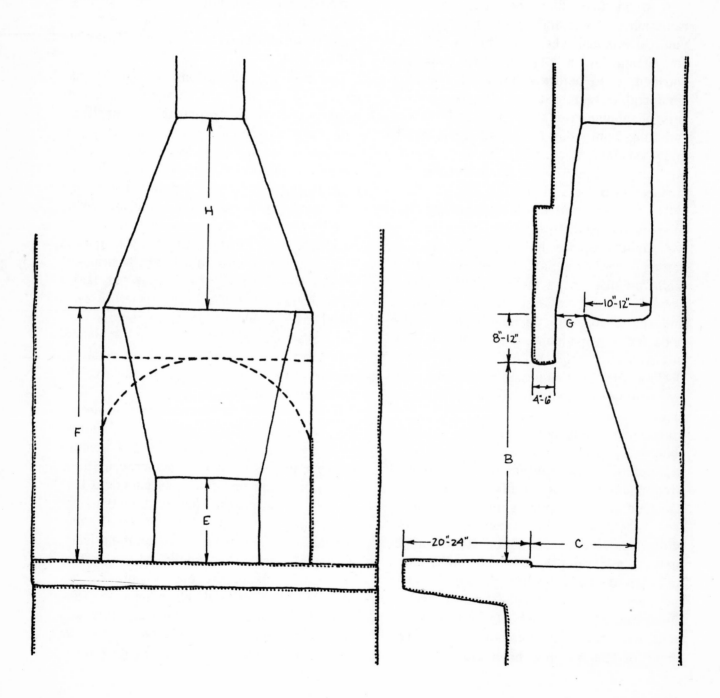

MASONRY
FIREPLACE
PROPORTIONS

FIREBOX DIMENSIONS

A	B	C	D	E	F	G	H
24	22-24	16	14	9½	33	4	~22
32	30-32	17	16	9½	38	5	~29
36	32-36	18	18	14	43	5	~32
42	36-42	18	22	14	48	5	~37
48	42-48	19	24	14	52	5	~42

based on use of firebrick dimensions 4½" x 9" x 2½"

Footing

Built largely of masonry, weighing six to seven tons, the typical one-story fireplace and chimney is perhaps the heaviest part of a house. Its height-to-base ratio makes it a tall, spindly structure at best. For these reasons, it is important to establish the fireplace on firm ground. When excavating for its footing, dig through top soil and all organic matter to reach a firm subsoil or rock base. All roots should be completely removed, for they will eventually rot and cause soil around them to shift, leaving cavities in the earth under the footing.

Beware of water running both above and below ground in proximity to your fireplace site. As you excavate for your footing, if the ground becomes soggy or fills with water, it is likely that this site will not support your fireplace. Also be alert for signs of ground (or subterranean) sources of water. A fireplace located over an underground stream may be undermined if the soil beneath the site is, in time, washed away.

Freezing and thawing also contribute to ground movement, and even the weight of a fireplace cannot counteract this force. Therefore, excavate for the fireplace footing below the frost line predictable for your area. In southern states, the earth seldom freezes below 12 inches, while in northern states, it is necessary to dig four or five feet to reach a depth secure from upheaval by severe cold.

The footing, made of poured concrete and built to distribute the weight of the fireplace over the entire area of its site, should be strong and monolithic. It should extend no less than 6 inches beyond all sides of the fireplace it will support. The larger the footing, the more effectively it will distribute its weight load. It should be at least 12 inches thick, and on soil of unquestionable stability, 16 inches is preferable to insure adequate support.

Different soil conditions require different types of fireplace footing. To build on rock requires minimal footing. To build on clay or on ground saturated with water requires a footing that will span a large area in order to "float" the structure over the entire space. Such a footing prescribes a need for the tensile strength of reinforcing steel, or rebar, which is inserted into the concrete when it is poured, preventing its cracking from uneven lateral stress.

To prepare the footing, excavate its requisite size and depth. Its bottom should be smoothed and its sides dug straight. A wooden form is necessary only if the ground is so dry that it will draw moisture from the concrete. It is easier to pour directly into the excavated hole, using its sides as a form. Pour the entire footing at one time, for it is important that the concrete set as a single, monolitic unit. If rebar or steel mesh are used, cover the bottom of the excavation with concrete, place the reinforcment, and pour the remainder of the concrete. The

finished surface of the concrete should be level and smooth.

Concrete for the footing should be slowly water cured for it to reach its maximum strength. Cover the surface of the concrete with plastic, saw dust, or straw after its initial set to insure against its drying excessively. If you prepare concrete by hand, a workable ration for the mix is 1 portion of Portland cement to 3 sand and 3 crushed rock. Larger stones can be tossed into the excavation during the pour, saving concrete. If ready mix is to be used, order a mixture with a strength of at least 3000 psi, (pounds per square inch.) Mix the concrete as dry as conveniently workable to give it increased strength. Keep enough material on hand and provide sufficient time to complete the pouring in a single day. If using ready mix, it is desirable to pour both the house and the chimney footings at the same time. More information about footing construction can be found in our book, **Stone Masonry**, pages 92-95.

Base

The base of the fireplace is built on top of the footing and is that part which extends up to the beginning of the firebox. It is usually made of poured concrete, building block, brick, stone, or a combination of these. It should be completely filled with masonry. If block is used around the perimeter, each block should be filled with concrete to enable the base to carry the weight of stonework built above. It is also necessary to use vertical reinforcing rod in areas prone to earthquake.

The base may have functions other than just to serve as the transition between footing and firebox and to support the hearth. When the base must rise a full floor through a basement before it reaches the living zone, it can be used to carry flue pipe from a basement stove or furnace. It can also lodge an ash dump with access door, which can in turn convey an opening that delivers outside air to the firebox for combustion.

Most often the base is not visible, being under the house or behind the foundation. For this reason, it may be built of an inexpensive, convenient-to-use material, like concrete block. If, however, the base is visible, it is more appropriate to use a more attractive material, like stucco, stone, or brick.

Ash Dumps and Air Supplies

An ash dump chamber is desirable for those who wish to avoid transporting ashes through the house when the fireplace is cleaned. Instead, ashes are brushed through an opening in the firebox floor, where they fall into a hollow chamber in the base. Occasionally, this chamber must be emptied

through a clean-out door. An ash dump is advantageous only if its clean-out or access door is placed for convenient removal of its contents.

An ash dump has three parts: the chamber itself, which stores ashes; a vertical passage, which leads to the opening in the firebox; and a horizontal passage, which leads to a lower, clean-out access door. As the base of the fireplace is built and a convenient height for an ash dump chamber is reached, at least 24 inches below the firebox, build a flat, smooth floor that will facilitate its cleaning with a small shovel when the ash dump is completed and in use. This chamber floor should be sloped slightly away from the access door so that ashes will not accumulate against it and fall outward when it is opened. At this point, the access door should be installed in the masonry. It must be made of fireproof material and fit tightly. Masonry suppliers stock 8 x 8 and 8 x 12-inch cast iron doors for this purpose.

Build ash dump walls of solid masonry. All corners should be accessible with a shovel for a thorough, occasional cleaning. The walls should rise vertically for 8 to 12 inches above the chamber floor and then narrow to form the passage to the firebox. At the mouth of this passage into the firebox, place the receiving door, called the ash dump door, a product also sold by masonry suppliers.

The passage from the ash dump chamber to the ash dump door may either be built vertically plumb or rise diagonally to its opening. Its walls should be smoothly parged so that ashes will not catch on its sides. If the passage must be a diagonal one, make the drop to the ash dump chamber as steep as possible.

One of the greatest disadvantages of an open fireplace is its tendency to draw warmed room air up the chimney. This can be partially alleviated by positioning a vent to deliver outside air close to the site of the

fire. The fire will draw this air for its combustion, drawing less air from the room. There are many ways to deliver outside air to the fire. One way to do this is to insert an additional opening in a wall of the ash dump. It should be positioned so that ashes, pushed through the ash dump door from the firebox, will not fall through this opening. A screen placed over it prevents both coals and ashes from escaping in the event that some occasionally do come in contact with this air inlet. If you do choose to introduce combustion air for the fire through the ash dump door, it will have to be placed in the floor at the front of the firebox, not at its usual location in the center or near the back wall.

Combustion air inlets may also be provided either through openings in the hearth or in firebox walls. Care should be taken to construct these passages so that, in use, they will not become clogged with ashes or allow burning coals to escape the firebox.

Hearth

The hearth serves an important function, protecting the area of the room directly in front of the firebox from hot coals which may slide forward while the fire burns. A wide hearth is, therefore, desirable, and should extend from the firebox into the room by at least 20 inches, preferably 24 inches. The height of the finished hearth should not rise more than an inch or so above floor level. A short rise above the firebox floor will prevent ashes and coals from spilling out of the firebox onto the hearth.

A hearth, built a foot or more above room floor level, has become popular. Although this practice may be appealing to some fireplace enthusiasts, it is unwise to place the firebox at such height for the space below it will receive no radiant heat.

A better practice is that in which the fireplace is built **below** floor level, creating an area of sunken hearth several feet in width. This step-down hearth provides a convenient place in which to sit and bask, benefitting fully from the fire's radiance.

If the living room floor is entirely of masonry, there is no reason to build a separate hearth; the whole expanse of floor, in effect, becomes a hearth. If, however, the fireplace is to be surrounded by a wooden floor, a hearth is mandatory. One may be constructed in several ways, the easiest but not the sturdiest of which is built directly on the wooden floor. To do so, you need an exceptionally strong floor, perhaps one using double joists, extra bridging, and a rigid subfloor to avoid springiness. Floor movement will eventually crack any masonry laid upon it. Use a thin lightweight masonry material, like slate, paving brick, or tile. Most stone is too heavy and thick for this purpose.

Over the subfloor, place a layer of heavy

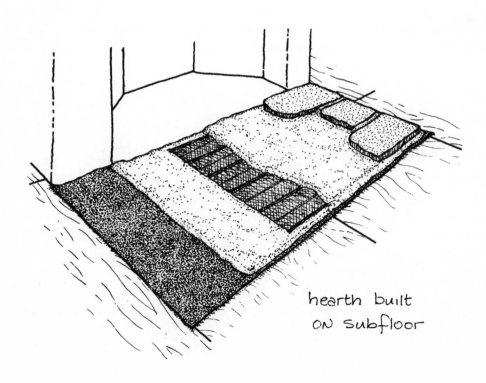

hearth built
on subfloor

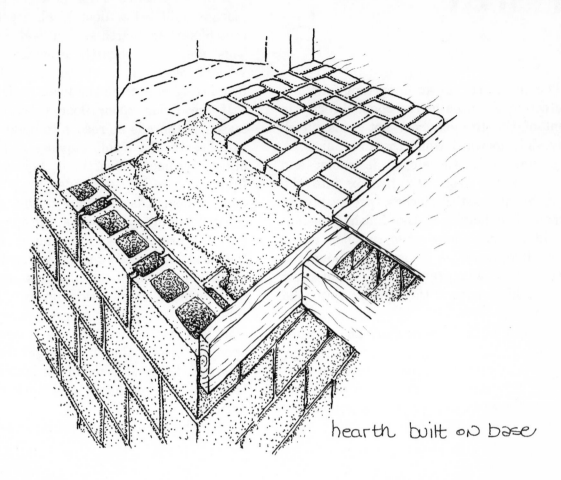

hearth built on base

building paper, foil side up. This protects the wood from contact with moisture in the masonry mortar. On this paper, spread a thin layer of mortar and into it embed high-ribbed expanded metal lath. Cover the lath with another layer of mortar, and into this bed, lay the finish masonry face. Compactly fill all joints in this facing, especially those in the area of the hearth which meets the firebox. This area is most vulnerable to cracking due to the intense heat cast there by the fire and from the differential settling of the hearth and firebox. It is, therefore, the area subject to the greatest fire danger if embers should reach wooden flooring through cracks in hearth masonry.

A stronger hearth will result when the base of the fireplace is built large enough to accomodate a hearth as well. By building in this manner, fireplace and hearth become an integral entity with no possibility of either settling apart from the other and making it possible to build and finish the hearth with heavier masonry materials. The base for this type of hearth is built to within several inches of the level of the living room floor and is covered with a smooth, level of mortar for an even working surface. The finish of the hearth should be postponed until the inside aspect of the fireplace is completed. This prevents spoiling the finish work, for mortar and chunks of masonry debris inevitably drop to the hearth while the upper reaches of the fireplace are being built.

The hearth should, however, be finished before the living room finished flooring is laid. To facilitate carpentry of the finished

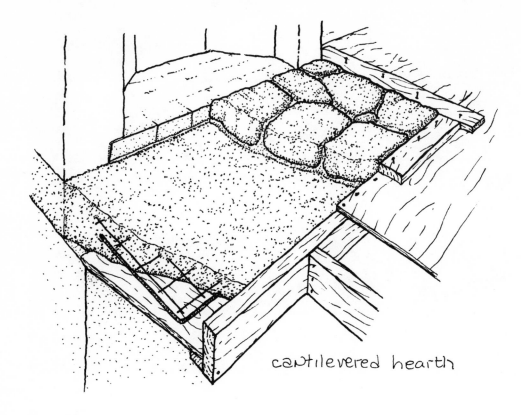

cantilevered hearth

flooring, build a framework around the perimeter of the hearth to the exact height of the floor finish. The hearth will be poured against this framework, and any unevenness or spaces in the brick or stone work will be filled with mortar. After the concrete has been poured and set and the framework has been ripped away, there will be a smooth, straight edge of dry mortar against which to build the flooring. This procedure should be followed whenever wood and masonry contact each other.

There is another method for building a hearth, one which cantilevers the hearth beyond the base. This method requires more preparation but uses less material than that needed to build a large base from ground to floor level merely to accomodate a hearth. Extending from 8 inches beyond the front of the firebox, the base is built to within close proximity of the bottom of the floor joists. The hearth is boxed in, using floor joists and a header for sides of the form. The bottom of the form is made of plywood or 1-inch boards and is shaped so that the bulk of its finished weight will bear against the base.

Into this form, concrete is poured over the entire area, to within 3 or 4 inches of floor level. For it to be strong and well anchored to the rest of the base, it is necessary to reinforce this cantilevered portion with rebar and steel mesh. Like the fireplace footing, it is important to pour the hearth pad all at once, enabling it to set as a unit. Its surface should be smooth and level. In several days, the hearth pad will be self-supporting and firm enough to build upon.

1. Wooden form built in place.

2. Ready to fill with concrete.

3. Concrete, rebar, and wire mesh.

4. Finished smooth.

Firebox

The construction of the firebox is the most critical of all tasks when building a fireplace, for its shape will affect chimney draw and the amount of radiant heat that will be available to the household. Since the firebox is that part of the fireplace experiencing the hottest temperatures of the fire, its construction requires a wise selection of masonry materials and careful craftsmanship. The firebox floor and walls of this traditional Rumford-style fireplace are made of firebrick, which are mortared together with refractory cement. In this instance, it is especially important to use these heat resistant materials, for to compromise the quality of materials for this type of fireplace will require its premature repair. The firebox consists of five surfaces: a floor, a vertical fireback, a slanting fireback, and two covings. The shape of these parts governs how smoke will be removed and how fireplace heating will be enhanced.

The floor. To lay the firebox floor, first determine its height, which should be approximately level with the finished floor. Lay out floor dimensions with string lines to mark the height, the front line of the firebox, and the center of its opening.

Firebrick is a porous material, which immediately absorbs moisture when laid in wet mortar, weakening the bond between mortar and brick. To avoid this, momentarily submerge each brick in water before laying it. Do not saturate the brick as you would a sponge, for it will "float" on top of the mortar rather than seating into it. On the other hand, prepare a bed stiff enough to prevent brick from sinking into an excessively wet mortar. Initially, trowel down more mortar than needed. Any excess will squeeze from the joint when the brick is tapped down to its proper height. Lay the brick tightly against each other — without a mortared joint which would disintegrate in the fire's heat. Portland cement mortar may

be used to lay firebrick for it will never come into direct contact with the fire. Use a level to ascertain that the brick are laid straight and true.

Because the floor will support firebox walls, it should be built larger than finished firebox dimensions. For example, if you plan to build a fireplace with a front opening of 42 inches, the first line of floor brick should measure at least 48 inches in width.

Accuracy and neatness are inseparable from durability. Make rows straight and plumb and build the bond with consistent spacing. Eliminate the solitary brick which blocks the passage leading to the ash dump. If you planned with care, this passage should emerge without interrupting the pattern of the brick floor. Before building firebox walls, wait for mortar in the completed floor to firmly set.

Cutting brick. For tight, accurate firebox walls, firebrick must be shaped to exacting dimensions. They can be cut in two ways: split with a hammer and chisel or cut with a saw.

To cut brick with a hammer and chisel and to achieve consistent results when doing so requires skill. A sharp brick hammer is needed, as well as a brick set (a wide chisel) and a 3-pound sledge, with which to hit the set. Use a pencil and a straight edge to mark the brick with the line to be cut. Place the brick to be cut face upward on a bed of loosely packed sand. The sand cushion will localize the impact. Position the brick set on the line and tap lightly, scoring the brick. Always direct the blow to strike slightly toward one side of the brick, away from that portion you wish to use. Score the other three sides of the brick, and then return to the face where you will rap the set sharply against the scored line. The brick should break on the line, although the break may need "dressing" or trimming. The larger of the ragged protrusions can be removed with the chisel end of the brick hammer. Smaller pieces of rough surface can be sanded with a carborundum stone.

To learn to break brick with this method requires patience. Do not expect to achieve effective results quickly. You may need to practice on less expensive red brick before attempting to cut firebrick.

An easier method and one giving more consistent results is to score firebrick with a saw. Abrasive masonry blades can be purchased for a circular saw. Although they can cut entirely through a brick, scoring it 3/4 of an inch deep is sufficient. Proceed slowly while cutting and do not overwork the motor of the saw. In order to see your cutting line, you may have to stop in the middle of your sawing to clear the dust that is created. Cut the brick on its face side. Then turn it over, supporting it in your hand with the palm on one side of the cut and your fingers on the other. Tap directly over the cut with the brick hammer, and the brick should break along the score line.

The walls. Firebox walls must be built with precise dimensions and angles to form the correct configuration for the chimney

throat. To do this requires accurate preparation. Be sure you have visualized all dimensions before you begin to build.

Unlike laying the firebox floor, the walls must be laid with refractory cement. Mortar joints should be as thin as possible, far thinner than the customary brick joint. The building code requires a joint of no more than a quarter of an inch, sometimes necessitating that the beginner mason re-lay brick several times. The extra care, however, is worth the lasting results.

To proceed, first mark the placement of walls on the firebox floor. Lay brick on the back wall, working from the center toward the side walls. Check frequently to assure that brick are level, plumb, and straight. Firebrick walls, laid with the large face of brick visible, are just 2 1/2 inches thick. Besides saving material, mortar joints are fewer in number, making for a stronger wall. Since it will be backed with solid masonry, the thinness of this wall is not significant.

Ash dump/air supply should be farther forward.

73

After laying the first course of the back wall, the first course of the two side walls is mortared in place, starting at the back wall and working forward. The leading edge of the firebrick wall will not extend to the front edge of the firebox floor, for you must leave room for the intersecting of the exterior masonry facing and the brick of the side wall. Build succeeding courses like the first, scrupulously checking that they are plumb and level.

When you reach a height on the back wall where it should begin to slope inward to form the chimney throat, you must know the exact angle of slope forming this passage. A wooden template is used to align the brick. To lay this slanting fireback, position each brick carefully at the angle consistent with that of the template, holding the template in place momentarily while the mortar sets. As each course of fireback is completed, lay side wall courses, moving from the back to the front of the firebox. The side brick, which butt into the sloping back wall, will have to be cut with a double bevel. Use a bevel gauge to transfer the angle of cut onto the face of the brick.

As the firebox gains height, the shape of the back becomes broader and the sides narrower. The top edge of the firebox is the point of departure which forms the back and sides of the chimney throat.

The firebox should not be built in exceptionally cold or wet weather, for the mortar will not set properly, affecting the bond of the brick. If brick become saturated, they will not bond to the mortar bed. To build on a hot day in direct sunlight is equally harmful. Masonry should be shaded to prevent its rapid drying, which weakens mortar. Do not hurriedly build a firebox; take time. To be done correctly, masonry work requires favorable conditions.

Building Around the Firebox

Eventually, finish masonry should be laid to the same height as firebox masonry. Since fireplaces are tall structures, as you build its finished walls you may experience difficulty with keeping corners plumb and sides straight. The easiest and most accurate method for establishing fireplace corners is to locate them with a string attached vertically from the floor to ceiling. Set these strings at each corner to define the shape of the fireplace. Sighting from one string to another helps to determine whether your work is in line.

If the fireplace is built completely within the house, you will want to work evenly around it as you progress upward. If it penetrates an exterior wall, you may build several feet outside the structure before you build to the same height on its inside facing. On the front of the fireplace, finish masonry is built against the front edge of the firebox. On the sides and back, there will be a space between the masonry finish and the firebox wall. This may be filled with block or mortared rubble. Whichever you

use, fill solidly and build for strength.

The exterior masonry facing on either side of the firebox is called a jamb. The jambs are built separately to lintel height, where they are joined to form the beginning of the chimney breast. It is crucial that the jambs be in line and level with one another at lintel height. The lintel is built straight across, spanning the space on angle iron permanently set in mortar, or it can be arched, using a temporary form to support it while mortar sets. While building the jambs, you should make provision for doors in the fireplace opening if you choose to install them.

The thickness of fireplace jambs and the lintel will finally determine the full depth of the firebox. For the fireplace to function properly, they should be no more than 6 inches thick. When building the breast above the lintel and across the front of the firebox, it may be necessary to construct a temporary backing against which to build. This backing can be made of plywood, styrofoam, or gypsum board. It is important that the back of the breast be smooth so that

Parging behind the breast.

smoke will flow unobstructedly through the throat. If necessary, plaster a coating of mortar over the back side of the breast. When the breast is completed to the top of the firebox, the throat is complete. This is the time to build the smoke shelf.

Smoke Shelf

Directly behind the throat is the area of the smoke shelf. It should be at least 10 inches deep across the entire width of the throat. Adequate space should be provided for the smoke shelf, for it will prevent downdrafts from reaching the firebox.

Forming the smoke shelf is a simple matter: smooth the area behind the throat with a layer of mortar. This shelf can be flat, although it is preferable to make it slightly concave. This shape is aerodynamically sound, catching and turning downdrafts of air or smoke. It also intercepts soot and rainwater, arresting their fall into the firebox. Water will be readily absorbed into the masonry, but soot will occasionally have to be removed.

Dampers

An essential part of the fireplace, the damper prevents room air from escaping up the chimney when the fireplace is not in use, and it regulates air flow while a fire is burning. For maximum efficiency, the damper should always be closed to the greatest degree possible. It is important that a damper close tightly and adjust to open at various settings. A leaky damper is similar to a window that cannot be closed.

Dampers can either be placed in the throat or at the top of the chimney. The most common practice is to insert a damper in the throat, just above the firebox. With this arrangement, the damper door is located directly above the fire for easy adjustment. When the door is closed, it prevents outside air from entering the chimney. When open, the amount of hot air escaping into the chimney from the fire is restricted, allowing more heat to enter the room. This door, in its throat location, acts as a baffle against downdrafts and prevents chimney soot from falling into the firebox. It is easily accessible for repair.

There are, however, disadvantages with a throat damper. Commercial dampers are not designed to fit a Rumford-style firebox. To install this type of damper requires a throat at least 10 inches wide. A wide throat in a shallow firebox does not permit the building of an adequately sloped fireback. Although commercial dampers can be altered, it is more desirable to design and build a damper to fit the 5-inch throat that we recommend.

When designing a throat damper, keep the following factors in mind. The damper must be built of metal heavy enough to resist warping by heat and corrosion from moisture and chemicals. On the other hand, if the door is too heavy, it will be difficult to

POKER CONTROL

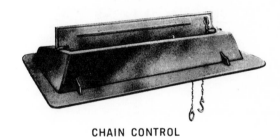

CHAIN CONTROL

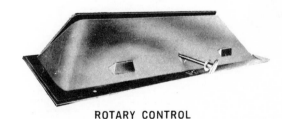

ROTARY CONTROL

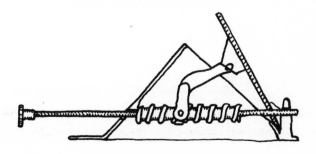

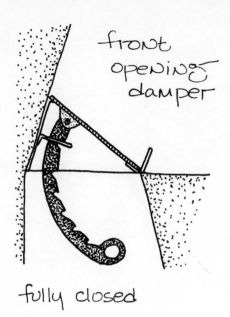

front
opening
damper

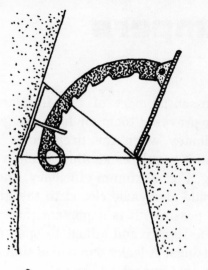

fully closed

fully open

OWNER-BUILDER DESIGNS

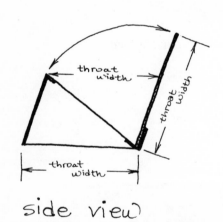

throat width

throat width

throat width

side view

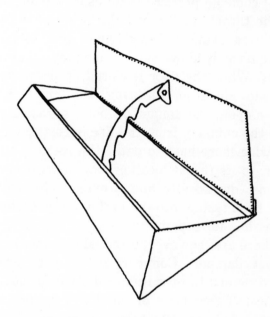

damper frame ~ top view

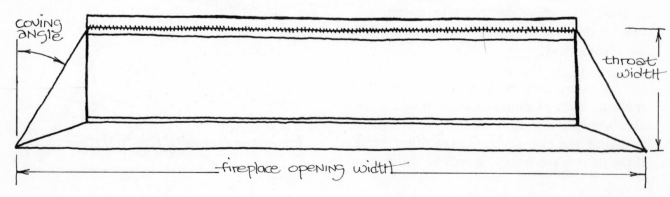

coving angle

throat width

fireplace opening width

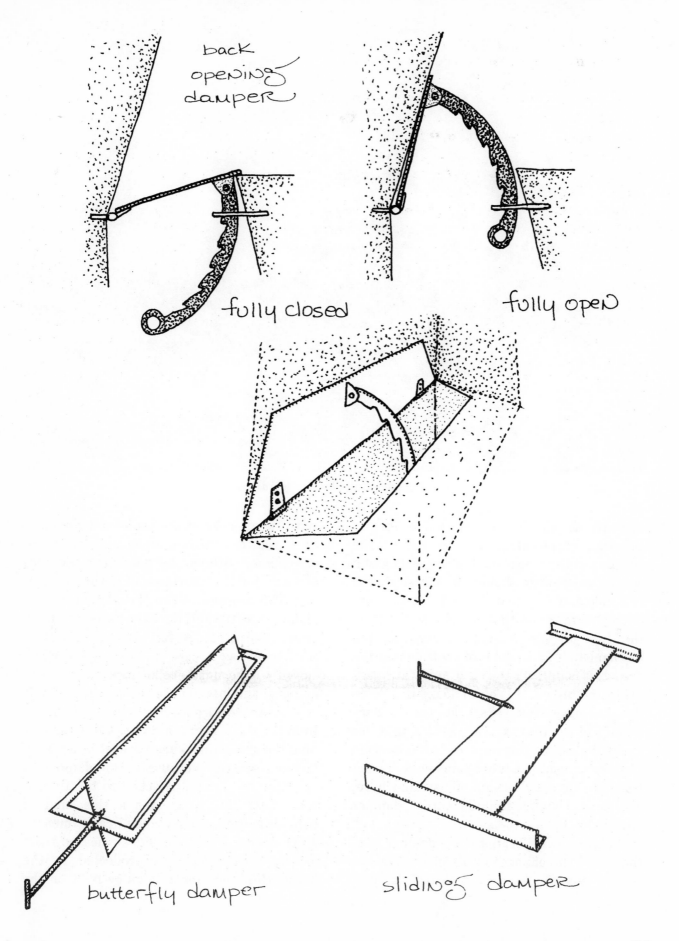

back opening damper

fully closed

fully open

butterfly damper

sliding damper

An owner built chimney top damper.

operate. It should be removable for its eventual replacement and to aid in the cleaning of the smokeshelf. The opening and closing mechanism should be built so that it is simple and easy to operate. It must be unobtrusive in order that it not detract from the fire or the masonry facing. If the mechanism is located out of sight behind the breast, it is difficult to reach, but if it hangs below the breast, it is often unsightly. Some dampers have a control set into the masonry outside of the firebox. This is desirable, for it eliminates dirtying your hands to operate the mechanism, but it can somewhat detract from the fireplace design. Illustrated here, are several simple-to-build throat damper designs.

An alternative location for a damper is at the top of the chimney. This placement has several advantages over a throat damper.

With the damper at the top of the chimney, the throat can then be made its proper size and shape, without the need to make concessions for the operation of a throat damper. The passage at the throat thereby remains unobstructed for easy cleaning of the entire flue area. A top damper functions additionaly as a cap, preventing — when closed — the entrance of rainwater, small animals, and insects into the chimney, and it is easy to service because it is accessible from the roof. There is no need to reach behind the smoke-blackened breast to adjust a damper control, because a top damper is operated by a chain attached to the firebox wall, near the jamb. When this kind of damper is used, the chimney draws immediately after a fire is first lit, for heated room air from the house has collected in the stack. However, for a chimney built on the outside wall of a house, there is a major drawback with this damper arrangement. Much heat entering the stack is lost through chimney masonry, even with the damper closed. A chimney built entirely within a house does not suffer this loss, for chimney heat merely dissipates back into the house.

Several chimney top dampers are available. Some are complicated and unsubstantial. There is one design, however, that is simple and long lasting. It uses a counterweighted butterfly door of heavy-duty cast aluminum. A similar design can be home-fabricated, but this model is well built and worth its purchase price. For more information about this device, write Lymance International, P.O. Box 6651, Louisville, Ky. 40206.

Expansion Chamber

The expansion chamber surrounds the smoke shelf and chimney throat and is that portion of the chimney where it narrows to the size of the flue. It is roughly the shape of a four-sided pyramid. Its front and sides slope inward, while its back, preferably, remains vertical.

Customarily, the expansion chamber can be built with red brick and regular mortar, for it resides well above the area of intense fireplace heat. Brick is laid around the periphery of the throat and the smoke shelf. It may be necessary to use an extra lintel angle iron to support the front course of brick. Even if a damper is installed in the throat, the additional lintel will relieve the weight bearing load on the damper and provide a flat surface for the first course of brick.

As you build around the damper, make certain that there is sufficient room for the door to freely open and close and for its removal when necessary. The sides of the chamber must, therefore, rise vertically until they clear the damper before they may begin their inward slope. The walls are corbelled; that is, each course of brick is allowed to extend beyond the one below. A 1-inch corbel will give the sides their proper slope of not more than 30 degrees from plumb. The inner walls of the expansion chamber must be smooth to prevent the fitful tumbling of smoke eddies. Corbelled brick should therefore be parged; i.e., plastered with mortar.

Brick may either be parged after each course is laid or after a number of courses have been completed. Mortar for parging is a richer mixture (that is, it contains more cement) and is slightly drier than mortar

Commercial throat damper and smoke shelf.

Expansion chamber built around damper and smoke shelf.

Narrowing the expansion chamber.

ordinarily used for brick laying. It is applied with a plaster's trowel or a square-ended margin trowel. To make the mortar stick to this surface, press it against the brick for several moments before removing the trowel. This supports the mortar while it bonds. Mortar will adhere to some types of brick better than to others. Do not use brick with a sandy finish; they are made to shed mortar. Instead, use brick with a textured surface so that mortar will key into it.

Parging can be a messy process, and

much mortar may fall to the smoke shelf. Remove it before it sets so that it will not stick to the shelf. As the expansion chamber builds higher, you will not be able to reach down to clean off this shelf. At this point, lay plastic or building paper on the smoke shelf to catch excess mortar and masonry debris. Leave the protecting sheet there, until the entire chimney is completed, at which time, it can be pulled out through the throat. Also, protect the firebox floor from falling mortar with plastic, paper, or by sprinkling sand on it.

Continue to narrow the expansion chamber at every course. This construction will remain strong and stable as long as all brick are well bonded and overlap at the corners. The height of the chamber should approximate the height we specify, but this height ultimately depends upon your design. An expansion chamber that narrows asymetrically will be higher than one which narrows symetrically. When it has narrowed to the inside dimensions of the flue liner, it has been completed. The entire chamber should have a smooth interior. Do not place the first flue liner on the chamber the day it is finished. Wait until the mortar has set overnight.

Once it is complete, face the exterior of the expansion chamber with masonry. As you build this facing, fill solidly around the chamber with at least 6 inches of masonry to give extra strength to its single layer of brick. This masonry fill needs to be thick enough to prevent the penetration of cracks to the exterior of the fireplace.

As the outer surface of the fireplace is built, it may be stepped or sloped following the transition from firebox to chimney. This affords one the opportunity for building mantle ledges, both in front and on the sides of the fireplace. Mantles should be stepped back rather than be allowed to protrude beyond the face of the fireplace in order to avoid unnecessary injury to passers-by.

Chimney

Above the expansion chamber, fireplace construction is easily accomplished by stacking flue liners and building around them until the top of the chimney is reached. Flue liners are recent innovations for chimney building. A hundred years ago, they were not available. Before they came into use, chimneys were built of red brick and were often only a layer thick. Such chimney construction has over the years, been responsible for many house fires. Creosote builds up on rough interior mortar joints of brick-lined chimneys and eventually catches fire. Too, heat or sparks from the fire can find their way through cracks in the mortar or broken brick to ignite wooden members of the structure.

Ceramic flue liners offer two advantages over this former method of chimney construction. They necessitate only a fraction of the mortar joints required for a brick-lined flue, and their interior is by-and-large smooth, offering easier passage for chimney smoke, improving draft, and allowing less creosote build-up.

Flue liners are available in a variety of shapes and sizes. When designing your chimney, check in your area regarding the availability of the flue size you will need to complement the size of your fireplace opening. The flue opening should be approximately one-tenth the size of the fireplace opening. Well built fireplaces will draw with a flue slightly smaller than this ratio. However, if in doubt about the design make the flue larger. The liners in most common usage and the easiest to obtain are those measuring 8 x 8, 8 x 12, 12 x 12, 12 x 18, and 18 x 18 inches. There are also round liners measuring 8, 10, 12, 15, and 18 inches in diameter, although, generally, they are not as readily available as the former rectangular-shaped ones.

The stated size of flue liners is similar to that of lumber sizing; that is, just as a 2 x 4 is actually only 1 1/2 by 3 1/2 inches, the interior size of liners differs from their stated, actual size. For example, a 12 x 12 liner may be 13 x 13 inches on its outside and 11 x 11 inches on its inside. Do not plan a chimney that requires a flue space of 144 square inches and expect to use a so-called 12 x 12 liner. It will likely be too small.

Another problem of flue liners is that they are often poorly constructed. Measurements vary, their shape is not uniform, and the top and bottom are rarely square with the sides of the liner. These imperfections must be corrected when they are set in place.

The first liner to be set should fit precisely over the expansion chamber. Lay a bed of mortar and carefully place the flue liner upon it. Flue liners are heavy. A two-foot section of vitrified clay liner can weigh over one hundred pounds. It takes two people to carefully lift it in place. In fact, with the fireplace at chimney height, it will be more efficient to have two people work-

ing to complete the balance of the project. One worker on the ground can hand up materials to another above, who will set them in place. Plumb the sides of the liner. If the liner leans too far to one side, it will have to be shimmed or propped with a shard of brick, and any gaps will have to be filled with mortar. Reach inside the liner from its top to smooth the joint so that it will not collect soot.

In some fireplace constructions, the liner may need to rise diagonally; however, the angle should never exceed more than 30 degrees from vertical. Although liners can be set tilted on brick, the preferred way to set them is to miter their ends so that they will fit together snugly. A masonry saw blade will cut liners for their diagonal placement, just as firebrick were cut. Liner walls should be sawn at least three-quarters of the way through on all sides before you attempt to break them with a hammer and chisel. After the first flue liner has been positioned, it is surrounded solidly with at least 5 inches of masonry finish. To improve draft and prevent creosote build-up, insulating cement may be used to fill between the outside masonry and the liner. But this is ordinarily not a problem for fireplace chimneys. For more information on insulating chimneys, see the chapter in this book about woodstove chimneys.

When the masonry facing has been laid to just below the level of the first liner, it is time to set the next liner. Lay a bed of stiff mortar on the inch-wide rim of the liner below. Carefully set the next liner on top, squashing the mortar down to pack the joint. Because of its weight and the narrow surface on which it rests, squashing the liner in place may push much of the mortar from the joint. Make sure the second liner is plumb. Reach down from the top and apply mortar to the inside of the joint, smoothing irregularities and filling gaps. If the two liners fit poorly, it may be necessary to re-

Building around the flue liner.

Cutting through the roof.

move the top liner and turn it around or turn it over for a better fit. Continue setting liners and building around them until they pass through the ceiling and the roof.

Flashing

It is necessary to prevent water from leaking into the house through the gap between the chimney and roof. This space is sealed with metal flashing and with counter flashing. Traditionally, non-corrosive metals, such as copper, zinc, and lead, were used for this purpose. Now, galvanized steel and aluminum are in common use. They are less expensive but require more maintenance.

Metal flashing is most often installed in two stages. A lower portion, called the roof flashing, and an upper section, which laps over the roof flashing and is called the counter flashing.

The function of the roof flashing is to prevent water that runs down the roof from leaking into the house. It is tucked under the roofing material and against the chimney. The counter flashing, on the other hand, is built into the masonry and covers the roof flashing. It sheds water running down the side of the chimney.

The roof flashing should be installed first, although it can be tucked under the counter flashing with minor difficulty. For adequate protection, each separate piece should overlap by at least 4 inches. Counter flashing is usually installed in steps; again, with pieces overlapping by at least 4 inches. It is embedded 2 inches into the masonry.

The two-stage method of flashing was probably developed for function and convenience. By separating the counter flashing from the roof flashing, the chimney and house are allowed to move independantly,

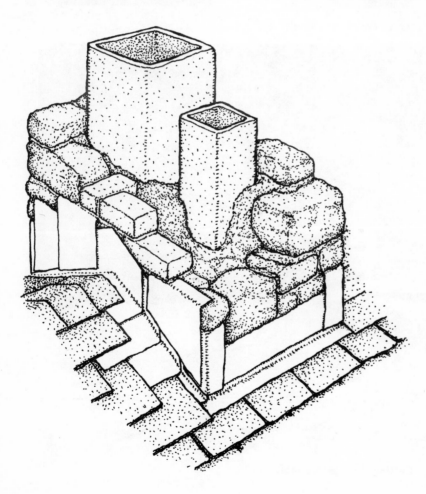

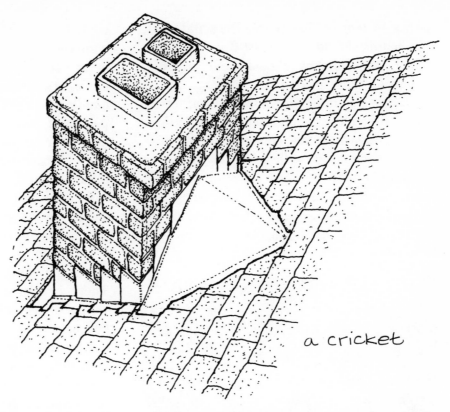

a cricket

without pulling the flashing out of place. In addition, in the construction trade, roofers usually install roof flashing and masons add the counter flashing. The owner-builder is often both mason and roofer. If he or she is confident that there is minimal danger of house and chimney settling, it is often convenient to install roof flashing and counter flashing as a single piece.

Corners are always the most difficult to seal against leaking. They require special care to assure that all gaps are covered. The area which must resist the greatest volume of drainage water from the roof is that side of the chimney facing the upward slope of the roof. To divert this water, it may be useful to build a cricket on this upper side.

Stone is rough and uneven and virtually impossible to flash. When building a stone chimney, the area under the flashing should be built of brick so that the flashing will fit snugly against chimney walls.

The secret of sound flashing is the tight fit of sheet metal pieces against one another. If this is accomplished, little or no caulking will be necessary. To achieve this, make certain that the pieces are measured accurately, cut straight, and evenly bent. Only a neat job will suffice. If you cannot get two pieces of flashing to fit snugly, they may have to be drawn together with sheet metal screws or pop rivets. Do not attempt to adhere pieces with roofing cement or caulk, for they will become unglued during hot weather. Silicone caulk may be used to seal over cracks, sheet metal screws, or rivets.

You can tell if a flashing job will last by looking at it. If flashing is neatly done with carefully made bends of metal and with little tar showing, it will probably shed water indefinitely. If cracks are smeared with roof cement, more will be needed every year to maintain it.

Finishing Off

How high should a chimney be? Tall enough for it to draw, should be the answer. A sound rule to follow states that a chimney should rise two feet above the highest point within 10 feet of that point. On a flat roof, this height should be at least 3 feet. At this height, the chimney should clear any disturbances from mixing air currents which could cause chimney downdraft. In practice, it is best to use an empirical approach: light a fire to see how the chimney draws. If it does not function well, you may need to build higher.

Lighting the first fire is always a suspenseful moment, even for the experienced mason. Before lighting a fire, give the fireplace its best chance to work. Remove all

obstructions from the chimney and open wide the damper. An effective test material is tar paper, which creates more smoke as it burns than the fireplace will normally handle. Do not burn the test fire for a long period of time. A fire of lengthy duration must wait until the mortar is well cured.

Light the fire and observe its burning. Smoke should rise directly upward from its source. As it approaches the throat, it should be drawn at an accelerated rate into the expansion chamber and up the chimney. If the chimney does not draw immediately, perhaps it needs time to become warmer. There are other variables to consider as well. For a fireplace to work well, it must be enclosed in a completed structure which has no cross drafts whistling through it. If your house is open and unfishished, the fireplace may function poorly; that is, the air temperature at either end of the chimney will be the same, and the draft will, therefore, be weak. Breezes may also blow across the fireplace opening, ushering smoke into the living area. Overhanging trees may cause the eddying of air currents. Trim branches to eliminate this problem and their probable fire hazard. If none of these difficulties exist and the fireplace continues to function poorly, then the chimney must be built higher. A taller chimney will create a stronger draft, removing the chimney top from the area of the roof which may possibly be raked with air turbulence.

Once the chimney's effective operating height is reached, its top surface should be finished or "topped off." In this final part of the construction, the last flue liner must be set level and plumb. Its top 6 inches should stand exposed above the chimney when all masonry facing is in place. This will protect the flue exit from swirling air caused by the chimney structure itself. Finally, make a drip ledge to hang beyond the chimney's sides to prevent rain water from running down. This drip cap can be ornate, giving

the last decorative touch to the fireplace.

The top of the chimney masonry should be smoothed with mortar to slope away on all sides from the exposed part of the top flue liner. This is the moment where masons often sign and date their work. If trees hover in the vicinity of the house, a spark arrester should be placed over the flue exit. This is simply a piece of hardware cloth with a mesh measuring one-half inch square. If a spark arrester is used, it must be regularly checked for creosote build-up. If you intend to use a chimney top damper, this is the time to install one.

The fireplace will not be complete until its masonry is cleaned inside and out. Mortar smears may be removed with a diluted solution of muriatic acid and water. Apply the solution of acid and water, beginning at the top of the area which you intend to clean, and use a bristle (not a nylon) brush of cheap manufacture. Rinse your acid-treated masonry surface well — and enjoy the results.

After a month in which to thoroughly allow mortar to dry, you may light the first fire of any duration. It should be small in size and burn slowly at first, while the last moisture is drawn from the masonry. If you initially heat the fireplace too rapidly, cracks may result. After a period of slow burning, the fire may be increased to full vigor.

The design we offer herein is the simplest fireplace we can imagine. There are, however, countless variations and elaborations which can be made, both inside and outside, on this basic design.

Materials List for 36" Radiant Fireplace Illustrated

Material	Use	Quality
Sand	Mortar, concrete	3 cu. yds.
Gravel	concrete	2 cu. yds.
Portland cement	Concrete	4 96-lb. bags
Mortar mix	Mortar	14 75-lb. bags
Refractory cement.	Firebrick mortar	1 large can
4" concrete block	Interior fill	20 blocks
8" concrete block	Interior fill	50 blocks
Red brick	Expansion chamber, exterior facing	1290 pieces
Stone	Fireplace, hearth	1200 Lbs.
Firebrick	Firebox	85 pieces
12" x 12" flue liners	flue	4 2-ft. sections
Cleanout door	Ash dump	1 unit
Ash dump door	Ash dump	1 unit
42" angle iron	Lintels	2 pieces
36" damper	Throat damper	1 unit
3/8" rebar	Reinforced hearth	20 ft.
6" wire mesh	Reinforced hearth	4' x 6' piece
20" aluminum flashing	Chimney flashing	20 ft. roll
Finished pine plank	Mantle	6 ft.
Caulk	Seal chimney sides	2 tubes
Muriatic acid	Cleaning masonry	1/2 gal.
Plastic sheeting	Cover materials, house opening	10' x 25'
Masonry saw blades	Cut brick and flue liners	2 blades
Rental scaffold	Scaffolding	16 ft.
Building permit	?	

Load Bearing Capacities of Soils

Soil type	Capacity [lb/sq. ft.]
Soft clay	2000
Firm clay, fine wet sand	4000
Clay, fine dry sand	6000
hard clay, course dry sand	8000
Gravel	12000
Rock	13000 to 75000

Building Schedule for Fireplace Illustrated
(Two workers)

Day	Task	Time Spent
1	Buy materials. Dig footing.	10 hours
2	Pour footing. Cut out floor for hearth.	5 hours
3	Build block base. Start Brick exterior. Form and pour hearth.	8 hours
4	Build firebox. Brick to hearth level.	7 hours
5	Start interior stone. Brick to smokeshelf level.	8 hours
6	Stone arch. Expansion chamber.	8 hours
7	Finish interior stone. Brick to top of expansion chamber.	9 hours
8	Brick to shoulders	4 hours
9	Brick to roof. Cut through roof.	6 hours
10	Install flashing Complete brick chimney. Install mantle.	10 hours
11	Caulk sides. Clean masonry Haul off trash.	4 hours
12	Return scaffolding Haul off tools. Clean up.	5 hours

Metal Flues

Metal flues are rapidly becoming a popular alternative to masonry flues and chimneys. Installed above fireplaces, they are either exposed to radiate the benefit of their extra heat to the room or they are boxed-in with wood. Here, we will discuss some of the advantages and disadvantages of this arrangement.

There are several reasons why a builder would wish to install a metal flue, rather than a masonry one. Metal flues are lightweight and can be quickly set in place, requiring no foundation nor any special structural arrangement. They take up less space than masonry flues and can, more conveniently, be bent or curved. Less skill and preparation is required for their proper installation.

Along with these advantages, however, you must be aware of certain drawbacks.

One thing to keep in mind is that no metal flue can survive as long as a well built masonry chimney. A metal flue must always be installed with the awareness that, in time, it will have to be replaced. Better quality stainless steel models may last up to 20 years, so their impermanence is only a matter of minor inconvenience. However, when replacement does become necessary, a metal flue must be accessible. Periodic inspection for holes and smoke leaks is also an occasional necessity. Framing these flues into walls, as is done by some of today's building contractors, is therefore an ill-advised practice.

Metal flue pipe is manufactured in a wide range of quality. The lightweight stovepipe in common use can be expected to last for only a year or two before it rusts or burns out. Even if rain is prevented from running down its sides, the water vapor in smoke will condense against flue walls and cause rusting. Such flue pipe is best used only to

A metal flue in a wood framed chimney.

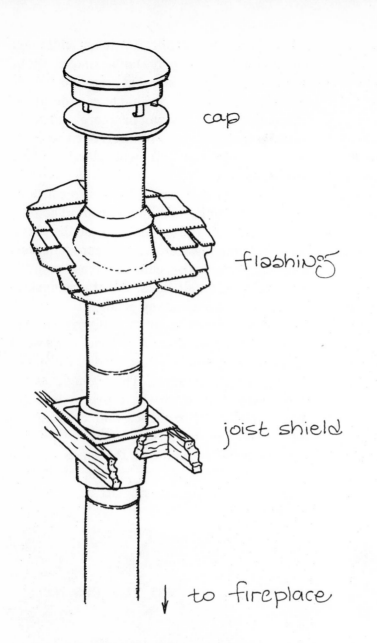

cap

flashing

joist shield

↓ to fireplace

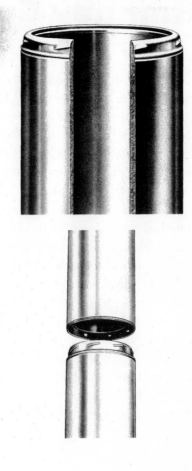

double walled
stainless steel
insulation filled
flue pipe

connect a stove to a masonry flue, where it is short in length and open to view.

Heavier pipe, similarly constructed, may also be purchased from a supplier and will last considerably longer than pipe of lighter weight. If it is used for many years, care must be taken to prevent the accumulation of creosote. Single-walled pipe rapidly dissipates heat, cooling it and causing interior condensation. When creosote catches fire inside a metal pipe, it can pose a formidable hazard.

The safest and most durable commercial metal flues are those made of stainless steel and containing insulation between double walls. These insulated pipe are less susceptible to creosote build-up. They do not get hot enough on their outside surface to be of fire danger. Still, these pipe are impermanent and require all of the previously mentioned precautions. They are also quite expensive, costing as much or more than the materials for a masonry chimney. In subsequent chapters, we will propose some owner-builder versions of metal flues used with air-circulating fireplaces.

Chimney Caps

Bothersome to design and build, chimney caps tend to look like an afterthought, continuing above the chimney's proper finish. Too, smoke curling unobstructed from a stack is appealing. Reluctantly, we concede that this device serves a useful purpose for some chimney problems.

There are two reasons why you may wish to install a cap over your chimney. The first is to prevent rain water from dripping into the firebox. Like downdrafts, moisture entering a chimney is intercepted by the smoke shelf, and during rainstorms, water may even leak into the firebox, carrying soot and odors with it. In addition, moisture corrodes the metal parts of a fireplace. If this troubles you, a chimney cap is needed.

Secondly, a cap can assist the functioning of a chimney. Sometimes in mountainous areas, in locations surrounded with trees, or atop a house with variable roof pitch, air eddies create downdrafts in a chimney. Even with a properly built smoke shelf, downdrafts can cause what is called "back-puffing." A similar problem can occur in chimneys carrying two or more flues. In some cases, one flue will interrupt the draw of the other. A cap will alleviate this situation.

There are a number of factors to consider when designing a chimney cap. The cap extend beyond the upper edge of the chimney and shed water. If the cap functions only to protect the chimney from rain, it may be open on all sides. But if it is designed to improve chimney draft, it must be built in a different manner. This type of cap should be tunnel-shaped, with its ends open to prevailing winds. Closed sides will block errant cross breezes. This tunnel shape directs wind through the cap in a straight line, molifying turbulence and creating an atomizer effect over the top of the flue. For maximum effectiveness, the ends of the tunnel should be as big, but not much bigger, than the flue opening. If several flues

occupy the chimney, it may be necessary to separate them with a wall, or wythe, so that their separate drafts do not disturb each other.

When designing the chimney cap, plan for the eventual cleaning of the flue. The cap may either be made removable or its opening must be positioned for insertion of the necessary cleaning devices. It must also harmonize architectually with the chimney, following the lines of the stack but not overpowering it. Within these limits, there is possible a wide range of design; a place where the mason's imagination, individuality, and sense of design may be expressed.

A cap may be made of masonry or metal. Masonry has the advantage of being permanent but the disadvantage of being weighty and cumbersome. Therefore, it may be formed and poured in place. If you precast a masonry cap on the ground, be sure it is not too heavy to be transported to the roof.

Metal chimney caps have the advantage of being lighter and easier to install and remove. However, it is harder to make an attractive metal cap. If you decide to use one, be sure it is well built and anchored to withstand strong winds. Paint it to resist rust. If you want a cap that is not visible, the chimney top damper, mentioned previously, may suffice. Although when open it will not keep out rainwater and downdrafts, when closed it has the advantage of discouraging entry by weather, insects, and small animals.

There is a large variety of manufactured chimney caps available, both metal and masonry. It is claimed by makers of some sheet metal caps that theirs improve chimney draw, but these are often ugly and simply do not miraculously make a smoking fireplace work. Ceramic caps are more tasteful.

Doors

What do you do when you want to go to bed at night and the remains of a fire still smolder in the fireplace? The fire no longer emits much heat, but the fireplace continues to draw room air up the chimney, like an open window. You cannot close the damper because smoke from embers must still escape. Aside from tolerating this situation, you have two alternatives. Either remove smoldering coals or block the front of the fireplace. For this reason, fireplaces need doors.

Despite their obvious usefulness, fireplace doors have only become popular in the last several years. The marketplace is now stocked with a large variety of glass doors, in a wide range of quality, size, and design.

Before you purchase any of these products or build your own, let us examine the features of doors which contribute to fireplace efficiency.

The primary use for doors is to prevent room air from flowing up the chimney and out of the house. Often when a fire merely smolders, a fireplace will suck more heat from the house than it will contribute to it. Another advantage of doors is that they conserve fuel by restricting air flow. If doors are installed in a heat-circulating design, closing them converts the fireplace into a form of woodstove or furnace.

The disadvantage of metal doors is that when closed, they block the heat of firelight from radiating directly into the room. When a fire burns briskly, closing these doors may be disadvantageous, for infrared red heat waves will not pass through metal or even through glass doors in any substantial

amount. Although currently in wide use, the only advantage of glass over metal doors is that, when closed, they give a view of the fire. Even this advantage can be short lived, for glass panes usually become smeared with black creosote and require frequent cleaning.

Most manufactured glass doors that we have observed are poorly constructed and operate with difficulty. The glass tends to crack, runners or hinges stick, and they leak air, as a general rule. Thoroughly inspect the glass doors you plan to purchase.

The alternative is to use metal doors. Although metal doors do not allow a view of the fire, they are stronger, easier to construct, will absorb and transfer some heat better than glass.

To build fireplace doors, you must contend with a number of matters. Air-tight doors function best. They are made air-tight by building them to close tolerances and by providing them with tight latches. It helps to build jambs for doors to swing against, and perhaps you should use asbestos rope about the opening to seal it, as is done in woodstove door openings. A fireplace equipped with an internal air supply will not require air inlets through the door. In this instance when the doors are closed, no room air will escape up the chimney.

The simplest door can merely be a solid sheet of metal lifted into place when needed. Of simple design and being easy to build, it is generally the tightest of all fire-

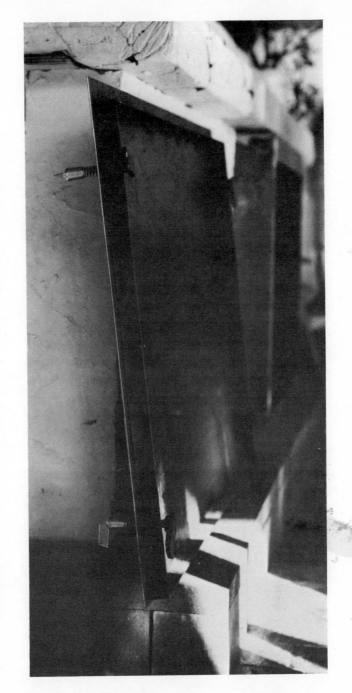

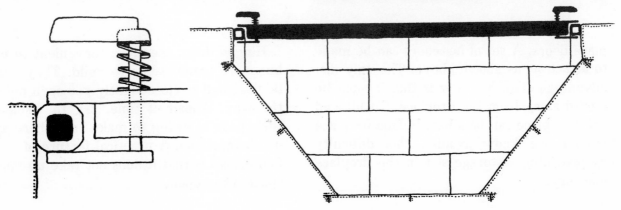

place doors. A set of fasteners can be made to attach it, as shown above. The only disadvantage of such a door is that it must be stored away from the fireplace. To lift and set it in place can be a hassel. One fireplace builder we know avoided this difficulty by providing a storage slot in the fireplace masonry.

Hinged doors are more convenient to use but more troublesome to build. They must be designed to close tightly yet open out of the way. Ahead of time, try to visualize their path of swing to make sure there are no obstructions. A practical feature of a bi-fold design is that it does not take up much space when open.

There are two ways to install doors. Hinges are placed into the masonry at the sides of the opening, or a metal frame with attached hinges is built into the fireplace opening. Be sure to use a metal heavy enough so that it will not warp with extremes of heat. One-eighth inch plate steel is adequate.

A third door design slides into a pocket in the masonry. This combines the advantages of the two previous designs, for these doors are both simple and convenient. They slide on a roller track, making their metal fabrication easier but the masonry work around them more complicated. Sliding doors are practical only if a wide jam is provided to contain the doors when they are in an open position. We recommend the use of doors when the fire is to be banked or left untended. When a fire is blazing, leave doors open to capture its radiant heat.

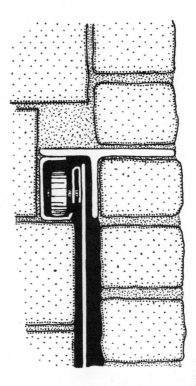

door mechanism

sliding door in fireplace

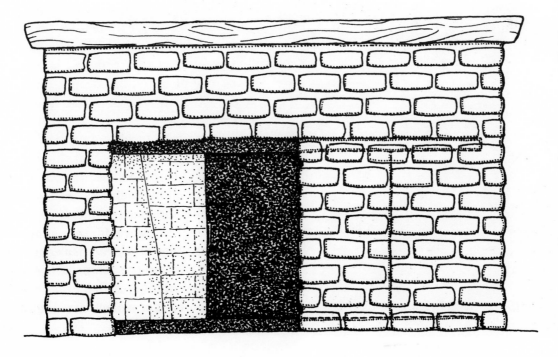

Grates

Census figures show there are over 20 million fireplaces in the United States. There are probably also 20 million different devices for raising the fire out of its ashes. A fireplace is not considered complete unless it is equipped with some form of grate or andiron. Although often taken for granted, this device can be an important addition to the proper functioning of the fireplace.

A grate, properly constructed, will not only support logs but will enable you to start a fire more easily and to maintain an even burning of the wood. In addition, a well designed grate helps to arrange logs so that they can radiate a maximum amount of the heat produced into the room.

To understand sensible grate design, you must first understand how wood burns. Fire occurs when wood and oxygen are raised to a temperature that permits their combustion. Fires are generally kindled with small

pieces of wood, whose temperature is easily raised to the degree at which they ignite. Once kindling is set aflame, it may, in turn, be used to heat larger logs to their temperature of combustion.

As the surface of a fair-sized log is heated, it dries — releasing its moisture as water vapor. It then begins to char as gases and tars, generated in the wood, are emitted. When these gases reach a temperature of 1100 degrees Farenheit, they will burst into flame. Combustion is that point of ignition at which the gases combine chemically with the oxygen of air around the wood. In ideal circumstances, they form water and carbon dioxide and release energy, which is felt as heat and seen as light. This increased heat, which reaches 2000 degrees Farenheit, further develops the process, generating additional gases from the wood.

Oxygen cannot reach the surface of wood fuel and cause it to burn until this flow of gases and tars substantially decreases. By the time it does, wood is reduced to charcoal, which is largely carbon and burns with little or no flame. Since charcoal insulates better than wood, heat penetrates it more slowly so that it burns at a slower, more steady rate. Once the process is complete, only ash, a non-combustible residue, remains. The foregoing is a sketchy, simplified account of this complex subject. For a more complete explanation, see Jay Shelton's excellent book, **The Woodburner's Encyclopedia.**

To kindle a briskly burning fire, wood must be arranged so that burning pieces will keep each other hot, yet have sufficient spacing to allow them access to oxygen. A smoldering log rarely ignites its own combustible gases, since for its complete combustion it must be placed near enough to hot coals to generate the temperature necessary to set gases aflame. A fire grate should hold logs in a manner to satisfy these various requirements.

In actual fact, the grate is a relatively new addition to the firemaking craft. In other times, fires were built on a bed of ashes, directly on the firebox floor. Generally, a large green log was placed at the rear of the firebox, and dry wood was piled against it. As wood near the front of the fire burned, the "back log" began to char, eventually generating a constant heat and limiting air movement to spaces between front logs.

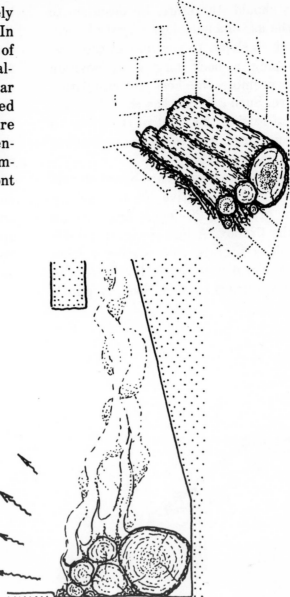

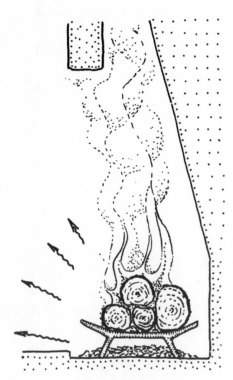

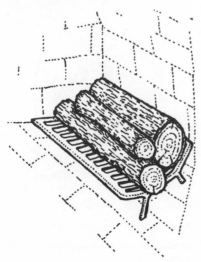

By raising wood fuel above firebox ashes, a grate increases burning efficiency by making oxygen more available to the underneath side of the fire. However, an improperly designed grate may foster undesirable side effects. Eliminating the back log will permit excessive amounts of air to rush through the fire, creating a current which can force rising smoke to billow into the room. Excessive air circulation also creates a "cooler," less efficient fire and prevents the firebox walls from reaching maximum temperature.

Grates should, therefore, be designed to include the use of a back log. A grate is preferable which slopes to the rear of the firebox, keeping a back long in a position that will promote the best air circulation for the fire. Such a design has the added advantage of raising the front of the grate to expose the fire's source of most intense heat, its burning coals.

Numerous grate designs are based on this principle. A conservative design simply slopes the grate at a 30-degree angle to the rear of the firebox. A less conventional design provides a grate with a more radical slope and two, distinct grate levels. At the lower level, a fire is kindled. Soon, it ignites larger logs above it. As these logs burn, they slowly slide to the back of the grate and new logs replace them, in a manner not unlike a toothpick dispenser.

If you buy a commercial grate, check its design and construction. Cast iron models tend to break when heavy logs are thrown on them. Those using steel rod must be made of stout material if they are to last for many years. A grate made of 1-inch reinforcing rod will burn out in 10 years. Grates are easy to build so this should be considered as an option as opposed to buying one. Some owner-builder designs are presented here.

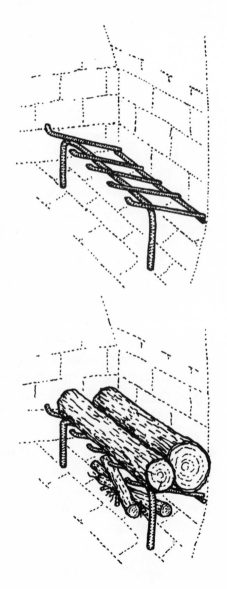

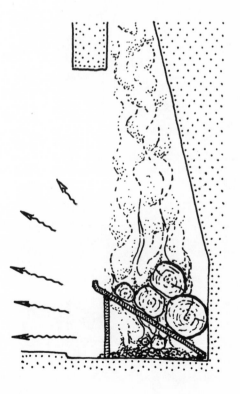

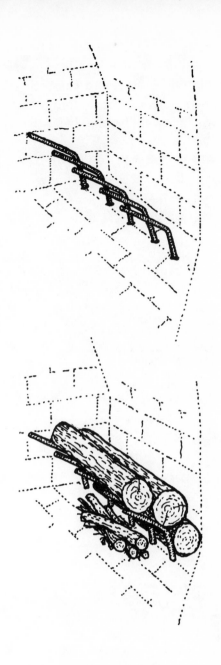

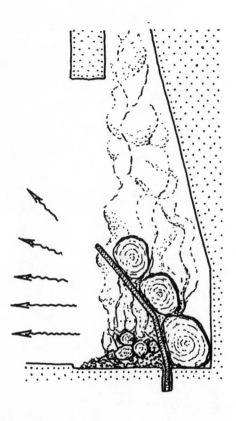

Hollow tube grates are another innovation that have recently become popular. These tubes curl around the fire. Air enters them at the bottom, is heated, and emerges from the top. Manufacturers claim these devices will double fireplace heat output when equipped with a blower. We are not impressed with these mechanical gadgets. Besides being ugly, they have the distinct disadvantage of cooling the fire and causing it to burn less efficiently. Although they do contribute additional heat compared to the output of a conventional fireplace, we prefer a shallow, metal Rumford firebox, which can do a comparable job more esthetically.

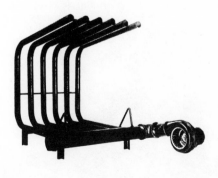

Pipe Products Company's Energy Grate

Air Circulating Fireplaces

Our previous chapter describes a fireplace which radiates heat from its open fire and a heat-reflective masonry firebox. Another type of fireplace captures still more of a fire's heat, which would otherwise be lost by its rise up the chimney. This additional heat economy is accomplished by circulating air through the interior passages in a fireplace, in which the firebox, expansion chamber, and even flue liners are constructed of metal. These metal surfaces rapidly conduct the fire's heat to air passing around them. This heated air then passes into the living zone.

As mentioned in a prior chapter, the idea of a metal-jacketed, hot-air circulating fireplace is not new. This fireplace design has been in use for centuries. It is, however, currently enjoying unparalled popularity due to the need for energy conservation and because there are few masons skilled enough to build an efficient firebox.

Hot-air convective heating differs in principle from radiant heating. Infared radiation from an open fire warms your body by its contact with the surface of your skin, regardless of the temperature of surrounding air. You, therefore, feel warmed because you are absorbing energy directly from the fire. With convected heating, quantities of air itself is first warmed and then distributed throughout the living space. Since warm air surrounds you, your body heat does not dissipate and you do not feel cold.

Actually, these sources of heat, whether radiant or convective, cannot be thought of as unrelated. To a degree, radiant heat does warm the room air and convected air does warm the body. The two methods of heating are, therefore, complementary and do not necessitate a choice between either system.

We consider hot-air circulating heating to be a desirable adjunct to radiant fireplace heating, not its substitution.

We, therefore, envision a radiating/convecting heat system that consists of a fireplace built entirely within a house and emitting heat from each of its sides. That is, infrared waves will radiate from the firebox opening, while warmed air will flow into the living zone from vents at the sides and back of the fireplace.

111

Manufactured Heat Jackets

To judge the merits of a manufactured, hot-air circulating fireplace jacket you must consider its design, its material make-up and workmanship, and its price. Generally speaking, this device is made of 14-gauge sheet metal and consists of an air cavity between the metal firebox and a surrounding metal jacket. Ventilator holes are located at the base of the jacket for cool air intake and at the top for warm air-exit. In some units, metal tubes pass directly across the throat where they are heated by rising flue gases; other models contain glass doors as well. Even the most inexperienced mason, following manufacturer's instructions can install these commercially-sold fireboxes. In fact, some units are made for what is called "zero clearance." That is, they require no masonry veneer; they are merely set on flooring and framed into the structure. Even their double walled, metal flues are framed in wood.

Fireplace built with a commercial heat jacket.

Owner built metal jacketed fireplace; air vents located on the sides.

Although these units are expensive, they require minimal expertise and labor for their installation. Their use, however, requires a number of undesirable concessions. For example, none of those heat jackets currently built employ Rumford design proportions. They are deeper in firebox and shorter in opening than necessary in order to reflect any effective amount of radiant heat. To mass produce these units, of course, necessitates their uniformity and, as a result, fireplace builders must adapt their air-circulating system to the limitations of the purchased product. This restricts the builder's options to a unit designed to meet the lowest common denominator of a variety of needs.

To lower manufacturing costs and reduce shipping expense, makers of metal jackets for fireplaces use light gauge sheet metal. As a result, it is common to find metal fireboxes warped by heat or burned through after 10 year's use. Although a metal firebox can be repaired when it burns out, most of these units also have sheet metal smokeshelves which, when rusted through, are nearly impossible to replace. The metal damper is another item often requiring premature repair, for its thin sheet metal door and its flimsy operating mechanisms will eventually warp and rust. Virtually inaccessible and built-in, they are exceptionally difficult to repair.

We conclude, therefore, that it is vital to carefully consider an investment in a commercially-built heat jacket. We feel they are not made to provide more than 20 years service. It may be a more sensible solution to design your own heat circulating system and to fabricate its metal jacket.

Heat Circulating Designs

To determine the design of your air circulating fireplace, you must decide the degree of complexity that you can tolerate in your system in order to gain increased heat efficiency. Plans must detail the routing of air passages, the amount of metal parts to be used, whether electrically operated fans will be installed, and even whether the fireplace will be combined with a central heating system. A systematic way to approach this planning is to consider these three, basic questions: where will air enter? How will it circulate within the jacket? Where will it exit? Let us consider these questions individually.

The intake vent should be located where it can collect the coolest possible room air. Its usual location at floor level alongside the fireplace opening is, therefore, inappropriate, since the air entering the vent has already been warmed by its proximity to the fire's heat. The vent should be as close to floor level as possible, but its opening is more suitably place on the side or at the back of the fireplace. The coolest room air is usually found directly beneath a window. When an air intake vent is positioned there

Commercial jacket raised with firebrick to gain greater lintel height.

and is ducted under the floor to the fireplace, the result is an even more efficient heat circulating system. Reduced floor draft is of added benefit. A further elaboration of this system is suggested in the last chapter of this book.

Once cool air enters the fireplace jacket, it must be routed through passages in order to be heated. These passages should be designed to allow air its maximum opportunity to contact hot metal surfaces. Therefore, a short, direct passage between intake and outlet would be insufficient; the best arrangement being a narrow, circuitous route through the double walled heat jacket. Metal baffles, attached across the interior of this heat jacket, create random passageways which heat air and conduct it to outlet vents leading to the living zone.

Customarily, hot air passages surround only the metal firebox; however, they are not limited to use in this area of the fireplace. The expansion chamber may also be constructed of metal and contain an air passage encircling it, making possible the recovery of heat from flue gases. Taking this design a step further, an air passageway may be built to surround a metal flue liner to capture heat from the escaping smoke. Each of these measures requires additional planning and metal fabrication, and care in building.

The final consideration is to decide where to position the outlet vents which discharge hot air into the room. These vents must be

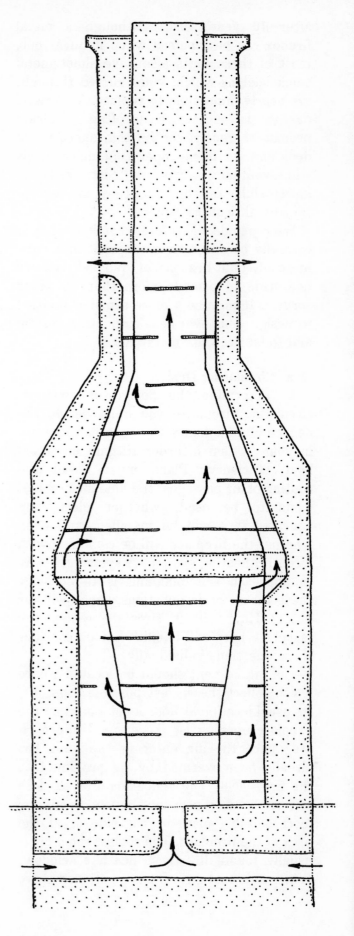

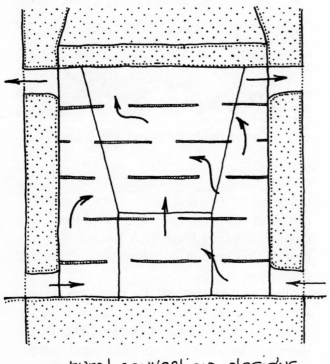

natural convection designs

carefully placed, for their positioning will determine how well air will flow through the system and where its heat will be felt by room occupants. If hot air outlets are positioned higher than intake vents, air will flow through the system by natural convection — which is the tendency of air to rise as it heats and expands. The greater the difference in height between inlet and outlet vents, the stronger the air flow.

Hot air outlets are usually placed on either side or directly above the fireplace opening. Again, this common practice is unfortunate. The area in front of the fireplace is already adequately heated by radiance from the open fire. So placing hot air vents there is redundant. Outlet vents should be set into the back and sides of the fireplace where the warmth of the open fire cannot reach. If the expansion chamber and flue are also to be used for heat collection, outlet vents can be placed even higher. In

Squirrel cage fan

fact, there is an advantage — to be explained in the last chapter — in which hot air outlets are placed at the highest point of the room.

An alternative approach places hot air outlets at floor level. From this vantage point, heated air can rise throughout the entire living space. It cannot, however, rise by natural convection because inlet and outlet vents are placed at similar heights. This necessitates that air be fan-forced through firebox passages. Although fans move air more rapidly than natural means, their disadvantages must be considered. They are noisy in contrast to the quiet state engendered by repose at the fireside. Because they occasionally require maintenance, fans must be accessible, not buried within the fireplace structure. Think carefully before you install a heating system that is dependant on the use of electricity, for this energy source most often fails during inclement weather when it is most needed. If a fan is to be installed, we recommend that it be placed in an intake vent mounted below floor level. In this way, it can be reached for repair, while it remains inaudible in the living area. Squirrel cage fans are quieter and more dependable than those with rotary blades.

forced air design

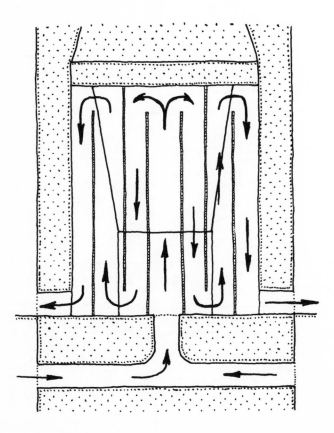

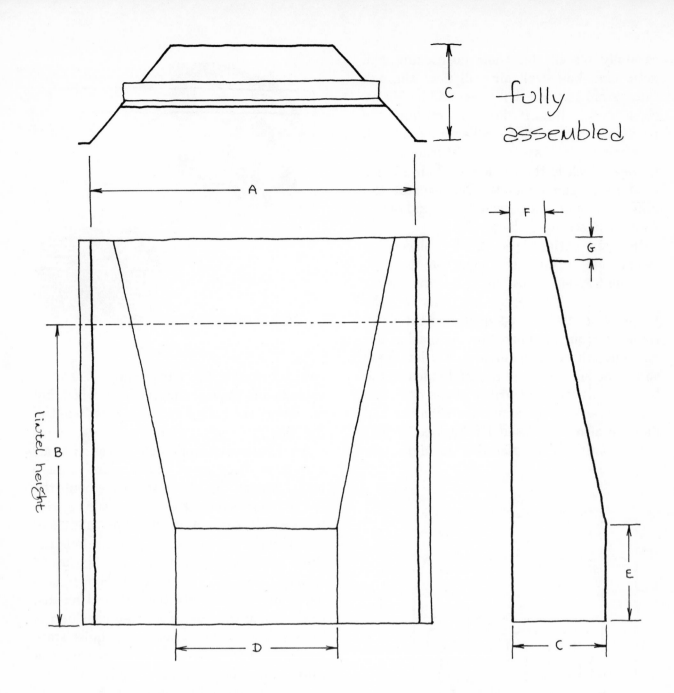

fully assembled

A Simple Metal Firebox Design

A	24	30	36	42	48
B	20-24	26-30	32-36	36-40	39-43
C	11	12	13	13	14
D	14	16	18	22	24
E	10	11	12	12	14
F	4	5	5	5	5

in pieces

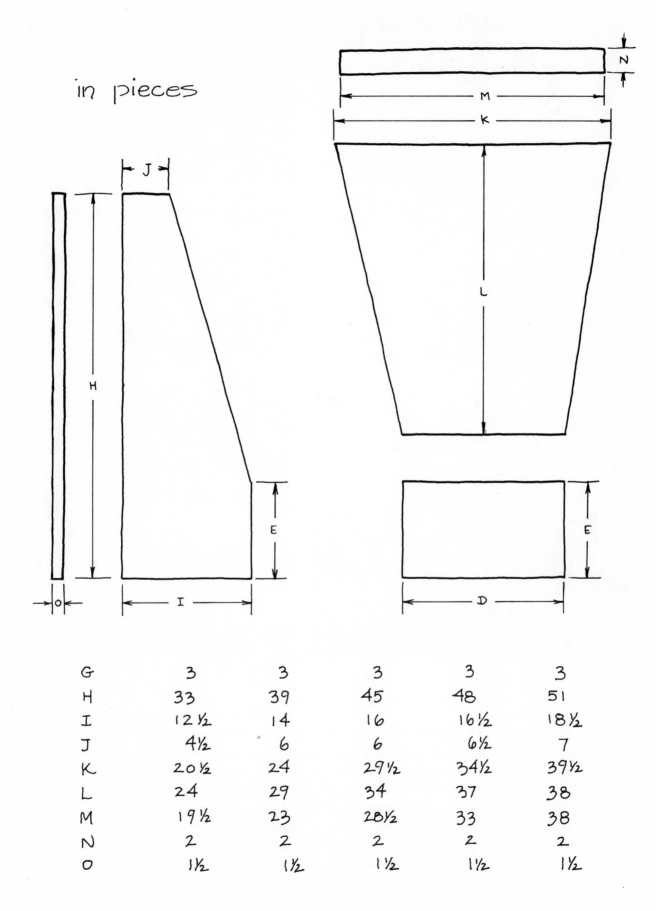

G	3	3	3	3	3
H	33	39	45	48	51
I	12½	14	16	16½	18½
J	4½	6	6	6½	7
K	20½	24	29½	34½	39½
L	24	29	34	37	38
M	19½	23	28½	33	38
N	2	2	2	2	2
O	1½	1½	1½	1½	1½

The Metal Firebox

A metal firebox provides a transfer of heat from the fire to air circulating behind it. In this chapter, we present an owner-built firebox design that can be fabricated by anyone with minimum welding skills at less expense than manufactured units. Essentially, this design is a metal firebox utilizing Rumford proportions. It does not include a metal jacket or a metal smoke-shelf. Air passages are formed by metal baffles attached to the back of the metal firebox — between it and a surrounding outer masonry shell.

This firebox should be sturdily built of heavy plate metal, which will resist warping and heat-scaling. We recommend using plate metal at least 3/16 of an inch thick.

118

This material may be bought new from a supplier or used from a scrap metal dealer for far less cost. If you do buy scrap metal for your firebox building project, be sure it is flat. Warped or bent metal makes accurate construction difficult. If you hire a welder, the extra time spent using scrap metal could amount to more expense than the material saving. Fabrication must be done with care and precision, allowing no possibility of air or smoke leakage between the firebox and the air cavity behind.

The firebox consists of four sheets of metal and additional smaller pieces, which act as tabs against which surrounding masonry will butt. The customary procedure for fabrication of the firebox begins with cutting the shapes of all metal pieces to

119

be used. A temporary base for the firebox is scribed or marked on a flat, level piece of metal, and the vertical fireback is temporarily tack welded to it. Next, the covings are tacked to the base and fireback. Check repeatedly during this part of the operation to ascertain that each piece is plumb and that the measurement across the front opening is equal from bottom to top. Often, at this critical time, temporary braces are attached to hold the metal pieces of the firebox in a fixed position. Following this procedure, the slanting fireback and then the two, narrow front flanges, and the metal support for the smokeshelf are attached. Once the firebox is assembled, all seams are carefully welded, excepting the base which will eventually be removed.

The following step is to assemble jambs and hinges for doors if they are to be used. Metal baffles can also be welded to the back of the firebox at this time, and if a throat damper is to be included, it may now be attached. Once the unit is complete, temporary braces are removed and the temporary base is detached.

Expansion chambers and flues should be built of metal equivalent in weight to that used in the construction of the firebox. Since these components are built into the interior of the fireplace, if they ever burn out or rust, it will be nearly impossible to replace them without tearing away surrounding masonry.

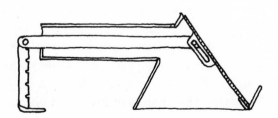 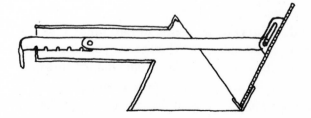

Note flue from downstairs woodstove.

Building the Fireplace

Like the standard masonry fireplace, the base of the heat circulating fireplace is, first, built level with house flooring. The only alteration of this base would be to place intake vents in the concrete, allowing air to pass from under the floor into the heat jacket passageway at the back of the firebox. The firebox floor is built of firebrick, as it is for a masonry fireplace, and the metal firebox is placed on top of this masonry base.

A metal firebox is very heavy and should properly be handled by two people. Center it on the firebrick floor, mark its location there, and remove it, being careful not to break or dislodge any firebrick. Cut a 1/2-inch deep grove in the brick flooring with a masonry saw, along the indicated location line. Finally, fit the firebox into the saw cut, making certain that the box is plumb and level and that the bottom of the box is firmly seated to prevent warpage and smoke leaks.

Now, build the air passageway behind the firebox. Prior to this time, the dimensions of this passage should have been determined and metal baffle fins should have been welded to the back of the firebox. To

Baffles omitted on this fireplace.

function properly, this passageway must bring air into its optimum contact with the hot, metal firebox. It should, therefore, be no more than 4 inches wide to insure the air's rapid heating and its rapid flow roomward. We recommend that the outer masonry wall of this air passage be built of brick set on edge. It may eventually be covered with a masonry facing.

When building the air passage, you should leave space in the brick for incoming cool and outgoing hot air vents at their appropriate heights. When cool air inlets are located below floor level, it is wise to remove several brick from the first course of the masonry shell to provide an access for the removal of mortar, which sometimes falls into the air passage during the construction period. Once the passageway is completed, these holes may be plugged, providing they will serve no further purpose.

When the outer shell of brick about the passageway has reached the height of the

122

String marks corners.

smokeshelf, masonry facing may be built around it, leaving spaces for the requisite outlet vents. At their terminus, these vents may be covered with metal grillwork for a formal, finished appearance. Or they may remain open as gaps in the finished masonry. Sometimes, however, a dramatic effect is created when stone or brick are laid on edge in these gaps. If you use metal grills, they should be substantial in order to support the weight of masonry above. We include herein some possible grill designs.

There exists an on-going debate about what constitutes the optimum size and number of inlet and outlet vents required for a hot-air convecting heat system. Some argue that air passage vents should be as large and as numerous as possible in order to stimulate the maximum volume of air movement in the system. Others feel that fewer and smaller vents will provide a more vigorous current of heated air movement. Both views are essentially correct, but the net amount of heat to be gained from this

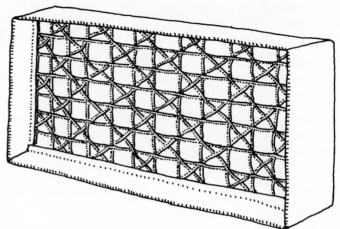

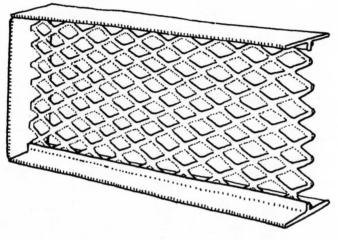

heating system depends more upon how well heat is transfered from the fire to air within the heat circulating passageway than on the number and size of its vents. In a system utilizing natural convection, air flow through the heat jacket passageway is determined in large part by temperature differences between incoming and outgoing air. The greater the difference, the more rapid the flow. Small passage outlets create an internal pressure which forces a vigorous movement of heated air out of the passage and into the living space, while larger outlets release the same amount of air, only at a slower rate. The size of passage openings, therefore, regulates the speed at which air flows into and out of the air-heating passage, not the volume of air or the amount of heat produced.

Fan-operated (forced air) heat systems work on an entirely different principle. In this instance, the volume of air moving through the system depends not on how efficiently it is heated but, rather, on the capacity of its fan. The volume of air flowing through the heat jacket is greater in this system; however, its velocity does not permit circulating air to collect as much heat. The net gain is about the same as the system which employs natural convection. The advantage of forced air is, therefore, not to produce more heat but to distribute it more rapidly throughout the house. Its fan quickly warms a cold room but is of less advantage in a room already warm.

We favor a heating system that promotes the slow, even circulation of heated air. Several large vents placed around the sides and back of the fireplace would be our preference. Placing intake vents under windows and hot air outlets at ceiling level has the advantage of directing the movement of heated air about the sphere of human activity, without creating floor drafts.

When building around a metal firebox and other metal components, it is best not to lay masonry directly against metal parts. Rapidly expanding metal will crack peripheral masonry, which expands at a less rapid rate. However, there are some areas where contact between the two materials is unavoidable. One instance of this is found at the front face of the fireplace, where the masonry jambs and lintel meet the metal firebox. We have found that when this contact is kept to a minimum, there is no serious damage to the masonry.

In the back of the firebox, masonry and metal necessarily, again, come in contact with each other to form the smokeshelf. The smokeshelf is one area of the fireplace in which we emphatically discourage the use of metal. This is because, unlike other metal parts, the smokeshelf has a horizontal aspect; its entire face is exposed to prolonged contact with standing water and to the corrosive compounds found in soot. It is inevitable that a metal smokeshelf will eventually rust through. Once it does, its repair will be extremely difficult.

The masonry smokeshelf is built by pouring a reinforced slab over the hot air

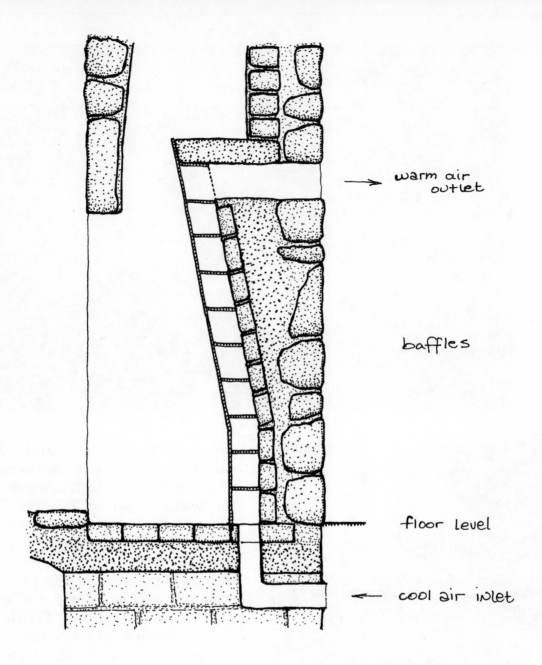

warm air outlet

baffles

floor level

cool air inlet

passage behind the firebox. Its construction is much like that of a cantilevered hearth — only, in this instance, the forming material which supports this poured slab must be noncombustible, for it is to remain in the fireplace for its entire existence. Corrugated metal, tin roofing, or ribbed, expanded metal lath is used for this purpose and it, in turn, is supported by a ledge welded to the back of the firebox. Rebar and mesh are used to reinforce the poured concrete slab, which should lie directly against the firebox in order to seal the hot-air passage from the chimney flue.

Over the smokeshelf, a brick expansion chamber may be built, as outlined in the previous chapter, or a metal expansion chamber may be installed. If you intend to use a manufactured unit and a metal flue as

The damper and smoke shelf.

Brick expansion chamber built.

well, build around them with brick, as you did the firebox. Again, let us stress the advantage of using baffles, which maximize the heating of air by its contact with hot metal. Remember, using metal chimney parts which cool rapidly can quickly cause creosote build-up, necessitating frequent cleaning of the flue. The chimney's ability to draw may also be adversely affected by a cooler stack temperature. For this reason, the flue should be of ample size.

Correctly built, an air-circulating fireplace should function exactly like an all masonry radiating fireplace. In fact, the metal firebox and its vents need be the only visible evidence that this fireplace heats from each of its sides, not just from its front opening. In this chapter, we have tried to retain the intrinsic appeal of the traditional open fire and to increase its heat production. There are other, more radical systems which attempt to raise the fireplace's efficiency to a level of rivalry with that of the woodstove. There will be more about these systems in the following chapter.

128

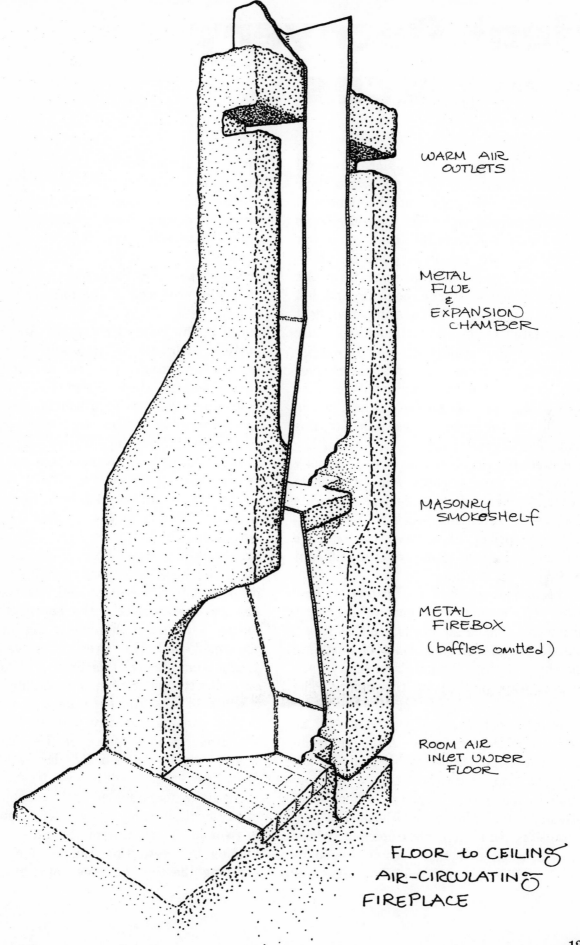

WARM AIR
OUTLETS

METAL
FLUE
&
EXPANSION
CHAMBER

MASONRY
SMOKESHELF

METAL
FIREBOX

(baffles omitted)

ROOM AIR
INLET UNDER
FLOOR

FLOOR to CEILING
AIR-CIRCULATING
FIREPLACE

Heat Recovery Fireplaces

In the two hundred years since Rumford and Savot made known to the world their fireplace improvements, untold numbers of inventive people have tried to devise ways to get more heat from the fireplace. In our mind's eye, we can even visualize these inquisitive persons contemplating the chimney's pull of warm room air and hot combustion gases — wondering how heat thus wasted might be reclaimed. To fully appreciate the amount of mental energy expended in these attempts to recover otherwise wasted heat, one needs only to review U.S. patents on the subject, which we did as background research for this book. The degree of these efforts is further indicated by the fact that we personally know several researchers who either hold patents on heat recovery devices or have a product of patentable quality. To understand the principles of heat recovery, we will now explore some of the thought leading to its evolution.

Throughout much of the history of fireplace development, the goal of designers has been to shape the firebox so that it will radiate the maximum amount of heat into the living space. Rumford's shallow, open firebox is a product of this effort. The air-circulating fireplace of the previous chapter is not a departure from but an addition to this endeavor. Although Rumford successfully achieved his goal, he left unsolved two crucial problems which continue to make the fireplace an inefficient primary source of household heat. The first of these is the large firebox opening, whose draw of room air actually results in cooling the fire. The second is the failure to recover that part of the fire's heat which flows up the chimney in the form of hot gases.

Advocates of heat recovery approach fireplace design from a position which differs markedly from that of other designers. They base their departure on the premise that only 20 percent of the fire's energy is produced in the form of infrared radiant heat, while the remainder is produced in the form of hot gases. Instead of putting their efforts into still other attempts to maximize the heat output of the open fireplace, these designers have each built what amounts to a simple, rectangular, furnace-like firebox that will generate extremely high temperatures. The heat thus produced is recovered from hot gases as they rise up the chimney flue.

The tall, shallow, Rumford firebox is, therefore, shunned by many heat recovery advocates. In fact, everything about this firebox differs from those mentioned thus far in this book, since, with this design, the purpose is to reflect heat back into the fire, **not** into the room. For the hotter the fire burns, the more thoroughly its fuel is consumed and the greater is its heat production. Ideally, this firebox should be only slightly wider than the pieces of wood it will hold yet sufficiently deep in order to hold a sizeable quantity of fuel. Its walls are properly constructed of firebrick, not metal, which too quickly dissipates the fire's heat.

Air-tight doors are an indispensable part of any heat recovery system. Their purpose is twofold. They control the rate of combustion by restricting the amount of air reaching the fire, and they also block the escape of heat into the room. For this purpose, glass doors are more effective than metal doors, because they do not readily conduct heat.

Combustion air is drawn from the room through air inlets in these doors or from outside sources that lead into the firebox. This latter source should, however, be preheated by its passage under or around the firebox to prevent its cooling the fire. An additional but seldom known source of oxygen is from the wood fuel, itself. Wood contains as much as 50 percent oxygen by weight. This is the reason why a wood fire continues to smolder even after all other sources of oxygen appear to have been curtailed.

Doors control the amount of air which can reach the fire at any one time, and they prevent room air from being drawn up the chimney. They are necessary, particu-

larly in designs such as this one, since it is not unusual for an open fireplace to entirely replace room air every ten minutes. Doors, which can close against a firebox opening, will reduce this replacement to about one change an hour. There will be more on this subject in a future chapter, along with designs for several types of fireplace doors.

In the furnace-like firebox of a heat recovery system, where temperatures approach those used in kiln operation, a grate is a hindrance. With much of the oxygen for combustion coming directly from wood, raising the fuel from its coals allows too much air to circulate and cool the temperature of the fire. In this heating system, the fire should be built directly on the firebox floor.

At this point in our discussion, we have what amounts to a small, deep furnace-box

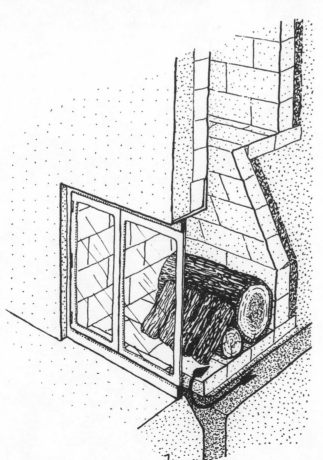

firebrick-lined to exchanger

insulation behind firebrick

outside air

that produces high temperatures from a thorough burning of the wood fuel. By using air-tight doors, we also have, in effect, eliminated the possibility that much heat will radiate into the living space. Most of this high temperature heat will rise up the chimney, where its advocates prefer to recover it.

Paul Sturges of Stone Ridge, New York, has invented and marketed a flue gas heat recovery system reminiscent of Prince Rupert's downdraft fireplace. Paul's Thriftchanger can either be built into the fireplace beside the firebox or can, he claims, be placed in the basement below. After they leave the firebox, hot flue gases are diverted downward into this device.

Termed a heat exchanger, this downdraft device is little more than a bank of 1-inch diameter metal tubes through which the hot gases flow, heating the metal. Room air is blown around these tubes to retrieve their heat, which is then forced into the room. In this process, the air cools the tubes so they can absorb still more heat from gases rising within them. From the heat exchanger, cooled flue gases are funneled back into the chimney and out of the house.

For this system to work properly, a strong chimney draft is necessary, requiring a tall, insulated flue which rises at least 24 feet above the hearth. To achieve this desired draft, the exchanger is at first

A Thriftchanger equipped fireplace.

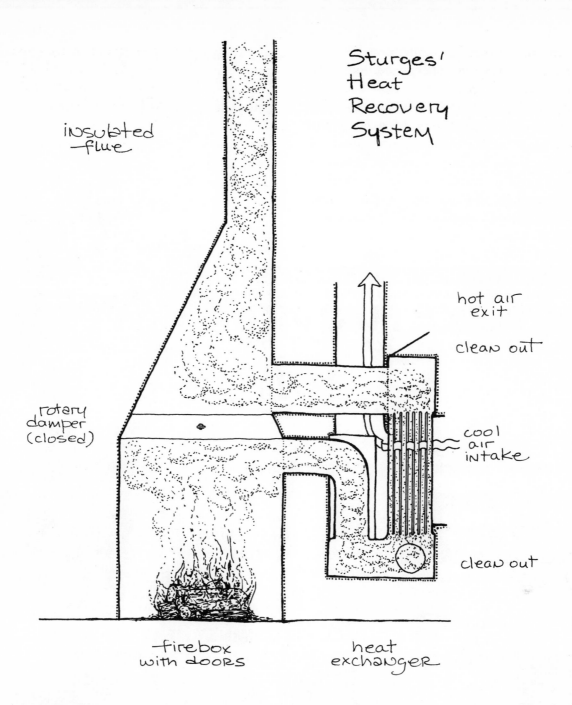

insulated flue

Sturges' Heat Recovery System

hot air exit

clean out

rotary damper (closed)

cool air intake

clean out

firebox with doors

heat exchanger

bypassed simply by opening the rotary control damper that allows access to the chimney proper.

Sturges admits this system can at times be temperamental, requiring optimal conditions to function well. Dry, well seasoned wood must be burnt in any of the metal heat reclaimers mentioned here, for creosote will quickly be deposited, clogging metal tubes. Even when using properly seasoned wood, the tubes must be fre-

quently brushed to remove residues. The high temperatures generated in the firebox compel the builder of this system to use refractory masonry materials to the point where the fire's exceedingly hot products enter the Thriftcharger. Sturges maintains that the savings in wood fuel and the heat gained far outweigh these added responsibilities. Indeed, when working properly, this system delivers an impressive amount of heat.

There are numerous companies selling heat recovery devices that can be built into a new fireplace or can be retrofitted into an existing firebox. Of the wide range available, each design purports to exceed the heat savings of its competitors. Most of these devices include electric blowers which increase convection of reclaimed heat. Although we do not endorse any particular brand, some typical designs are illustrated here.

A CHIMNEY-TOP DRAFT ENFORCER FOR SMOKELESS FIREPLACES AND EFFICIENT FUEL CONSUMPTION

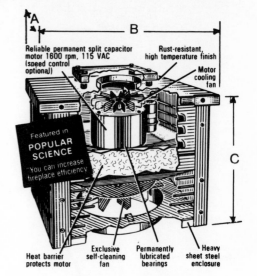

Reliable permanent split capacitor motor 1600 rpm, 115 VAC (speed control optional)

Rust-resistant, high temperature finish

Motor cooling fan

Featured in POPULAR SCIENCE "You can increase fireplace efficiency"

Heat barrier protects motor

Exclusive self-cleaning fan

Permanently lubricated bearings

Heavy sheet steel enclosure

HEAT HEAT HEAT HEAT HEAT HEAT HEAT HEAT
A TOTALLY NEW CONCEPT IN ENERGY SAVINGS, CALLED THE

FIREPLACE FURNACE
PATENT PENDING

MODEL FOR EXISTING FIREPLACES

Four (4) heat chambers each containing a triple baffle system. In short, heat chambers hold the air over the fire longer than other systems. Therefore, higher discharge temperatures, and being above the flame there is less chance of burning out from heat and acids created by burning wood. Fits any rectangular fireplace opening. Can be installed by home owner in less than 20 minutes. Gives you the luxury of a fireplace with the efficiency of a wood burning stove.

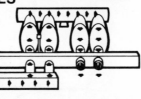

DESIGNED BY A BRICKLAYER FOR A BRICKLAYER

Better 'n Ben's
THE FIREPLACE STOVE

Boost fireplace output up to 10X

Glass Door ThermoGRATE® Unit
'Enough to heat a house'

Firescreen with Tempered Glass Doors Provides Even Heat Distribution

ThermoGRATE®

RECLAIM CHIMNEY HEAT with a FUELMISER

• ENJOY THE COMFORT OF FREE HEAT

HEAT flo

Converts your fireplace into a small forced-air furnace... increases heating efficiency by as much as five times!

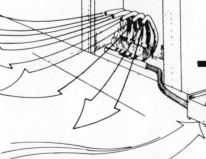

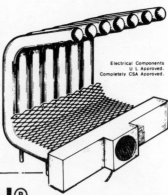
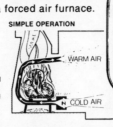

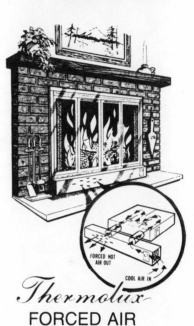

135

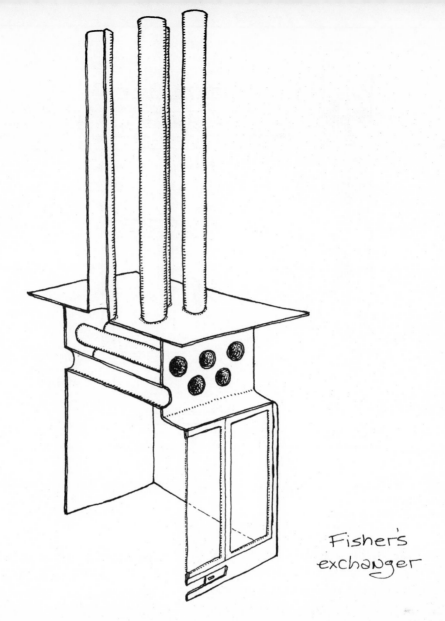

Fisher's exchanger

Another fireplace inventor is Jack Fisher of Auberry, California. Over the years, Jack has kept busy helping neighbors build and adapt their fireplaces to use his independently developed heat recovery design. When we interviewed Jack about his work, he flatly stated that, "Anyone who builds a regular fireplace should go to jail!" Unlike the systems we have heretofore outlined in this book, Fisher uses metal to build his firebox and flue. Again, glass doors restrict the flow of air into the firebox.

Masonry forms two separate compartments around these metal parts. The first of these surrounds the firebox, which is a rectangular, metal jacket. As hot gases rise from the fire, they pass around a series of 4-inch, metal, air-convecting tubes. These tubes traverse the entrance to the flue and open into the room. The second surrounds flue liners in the chimney; for, instead of using a single, metal flue, Jack divides the flue into five or six separate 4-inch pipes. In this way, escaping flue gases make their maximum contact with heat-transmitting metal surfaces. For evidence that the result is exceedingly effective, Jack says you have only to hold your hand over the top of the chimney to feel very little heat escaping.

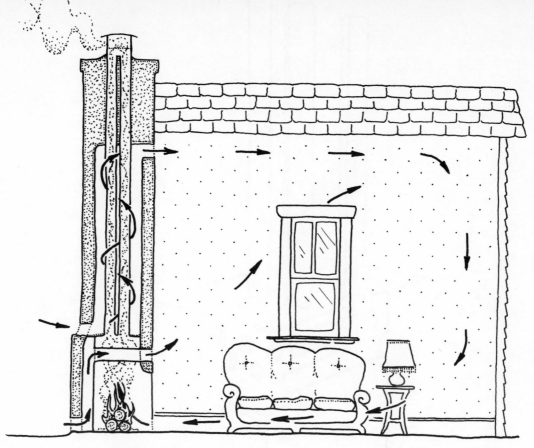

Fisher's air circulation system

A unique and, at first, disturbing feature of Fisher's system is that he deliberately introduces cold, outside air to these heating compartments. Jack explains that if you allow outside air to enter the household heating system through these warming compartments, it will not so likely be sucked in through cracks around doors and windows. Furthermore, cool air does a better job of extracting heat from metal flue pipes than pre-warmed air from the living space. Blowers are used when the fire is first lit but are turned off once convection is established. This system thus promotes the continuous circulation of warmed, fresh air throughout the house. Jack Fisher is pleased to share his heating system with anyone interested in it, stating that he is not concerned with patents or credit for his work. He muses, "I could have been a millionaire but what would it gain me that I haven't got now?"

One other heat recovery system we wish to mention is that of Arizonan, Bill Wells. The patented Wells Fireplace Furnace is another all-metal unit through which combustion gases traverse its 12-inch flue. Their heat is recovered by air circulating around the flue within a 16-inch-square jacket. Recovery is also made by air flowing through a 6-inch-square duct that runs through the center of the flue. Though it cools the fire, Wells feels he can also collect an additional amount of heat from air flowing through a hollow fire grate. This heated air will either flow naturally by convection from floor to ceiling, or it can be forced by blowers to flow in the reverse direction where it will emerge at floor level.

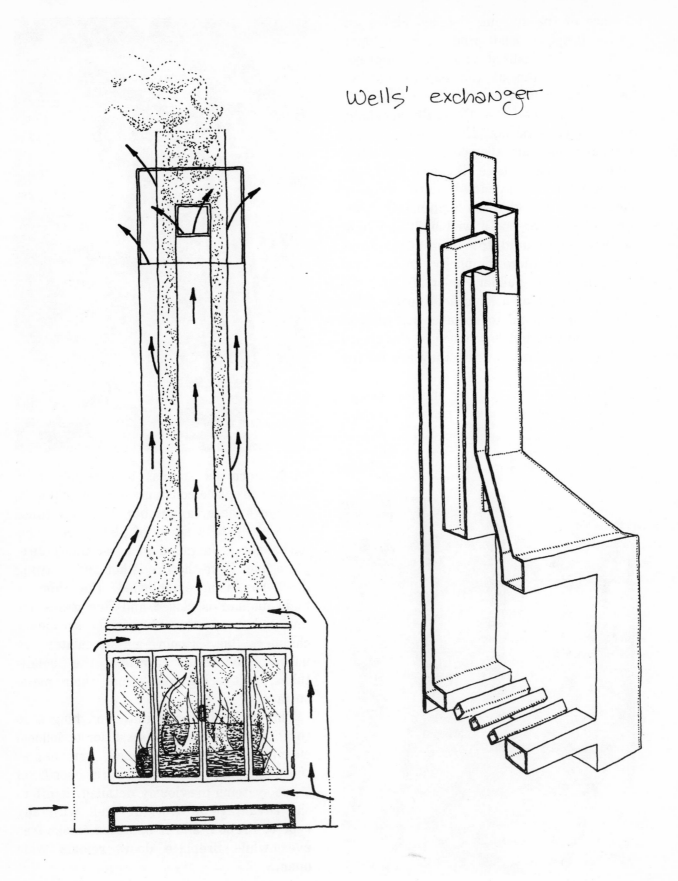

Wells' exchanger

139

Each of the systems detailed above improve fireplace heat production. It must, however, be realized that these improvements are often at the expense of experiencing radiant heat or a visual enjoyment of the open fire. Generally speaking, these systems do not draw properly when fireplace doors are allowed to remain open. Another disadvantage is that they are complex to build and require frequent cleaning. We might also legitimately question whether or not a well built, air-tight woodstove would perform the same function with more simplicity. In the final analysis, owner-builders must not only decide how complex a household heat system they care to build to achieve this kind of heat recovery, but how much of the charm and feeling of an open fire they are willing to sacrifice to do so.

Finally, we wish to offer one last design for an owner-built heat reclaimer, used

with enormous success by one of us in several fireplace constructions. In this unit, as shown here, a number of metal tubes are welded to a sheet of plate steel. This exchanger is installed in a secondary fireplace flue. Once the fire is hot and a strong draft has been established, the chimney main damper is closed and flue gases are diverted around the tubes in the secondary chimney flue. Room air circulates by natural convection through the hollow tubes, recovering heat from their metal surfaces.

This reclaimer is mounted on hinges so that it may be tilted outward for occasional cleaning. Although it may not be as thoroughgoing an operation as some of those systems previously detailed, it offers the advantage of working well with any type of firebox, and it operates smoke-free even while fireplace doors remain wide open.

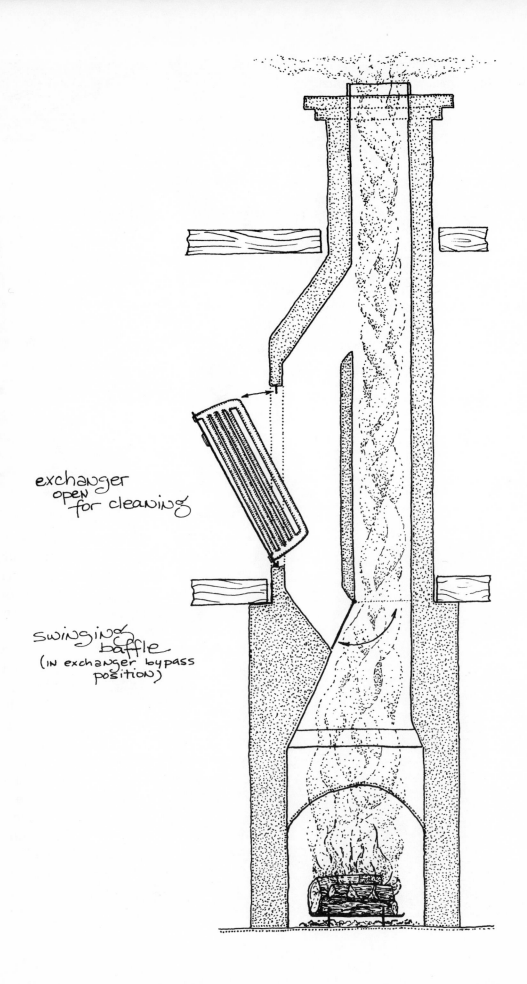

exchanger
open
for cleaning

swinging baffle
(in exchanger bypass
position)

141

Water Circulating Fireplaces

Every household should enjoy a year-round supply of hot water, both for domestic use and as a possible source of wintertime household heat. A home heating system using circulating hot water can be low in cost and easily built. It can be noise-free and dependable, operating even in a power failure. Like radiant heat from the open fireplace, hot water heat is more healthful to humans than that of circulating hot air, which often provokes drafts and is dust-laden.

The fireplace is an obvious, though surprisingly, little-used method for heating hot water, requiring the combined skills of the mason and the plumber for its installation. For this reason, the more flexible owner-builder has an advantage over the building contractor, who must build within industry-acceptable bounds.

Thirty years ago, in an attempt to combine space heating and water heating, makers of the air-circulating metal fireplace, called Heatform, sold an accessory water heating unit with their fireplace product. A unique but simple device which could be installed by any builder, this unit was nothing more than a coil of pipe attached to the rear wall of the metal firebox. Its sale, however, was abruptly discontinued a few years later — presumably because of troublesome units or faulty installation.

Building a hot-water circulating fireplace is a more complex endeavor than building an air-circulating one, for steam under pressure is volatile and explosion lurks as a potential hazard of this system. Therefore, this method merits an understanding of how hot water thermosiphons and of the associative problems of vapor lock in water lines and the need for temperature and steam pressure relief valves. Here, we intend to give the owner-builder some of the basic information needed to install a simple but effective system for heating water. A thorough course in the theory and mechanics of plumbing is, of course, not possible within the confines of this book. The reader is, therefore, encouraged to consult other books on the subject as well as tradesmen and materials suppliers who can answer questions we may leave unanswered and fill in details we do not provide.

Pipe Grates

A water-circulating pipe grate is the most essential and the easiest built component in a water-heating fireplace. One can be fabricated in a matter of hours at little cost. This type of grate is merely a serpentine line of pipe in which cold water enters a lower level inlet and exits, heated, from an upper level outlet.

To build this grate, you will need about 12 feet of 1-inch non-galvanized pipe — known in the trade as black pipe — and connectors with a 180-degree bend. A combination street ell and a right angle ell can be substituted for the 180-degree bend fitting. The 1-inch pipe size is recommended, because it has less flow resistance than pipe of smaller diameter. But this is important only where natural convection is to be relied upon.

Since water constantly circulates through the grate, the pipe never exceeds a temperature of 250 degrees Farenheit. Water absorbs heat from the pipe and prevents its damage by the same token that a Dixie cup full of water will not burn.

This pipe grate may be tied in with the house domestic hot water supply, without the need for pumps or extra wiring, if the hot water storage tank is placed at a position above the fireplace. Heated water can then thermosiphon from the grate into this tank, which is a standard, commercial hot water tank, adapted to your system. Thermostatically activated, this auxiliary heating unit is fired by gas, oil, or electricity when the fireplace is not in use.

As illustrated in the accompanying draw-

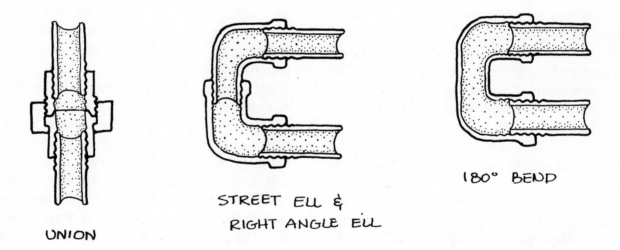

UNION

STREET ELL &
RIGHT ANGLE ELL

180° BEND

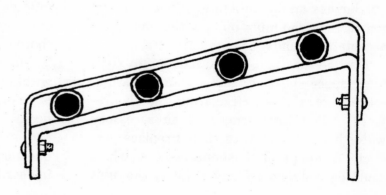

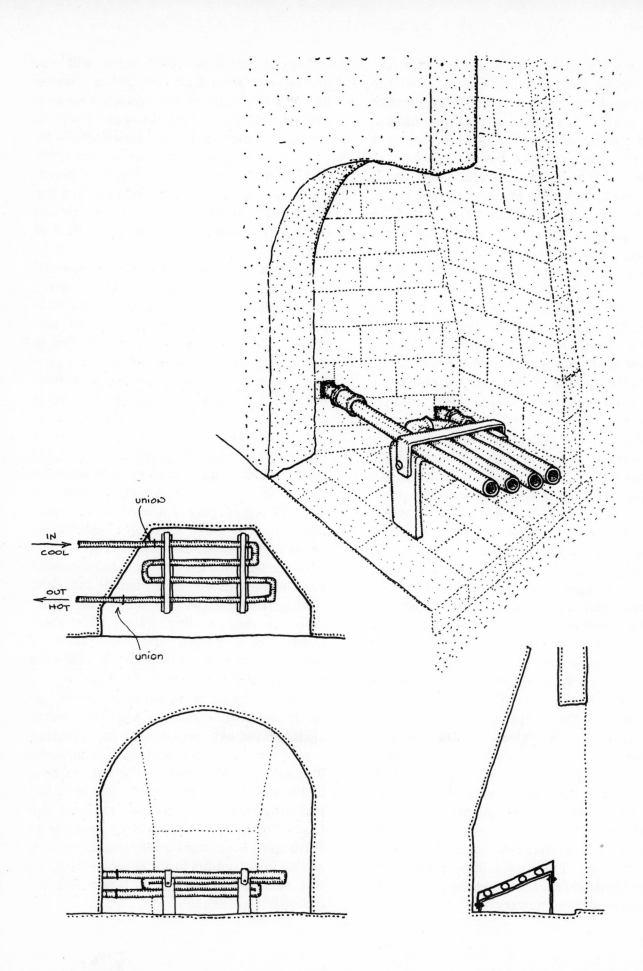

IN
COOL

OUT
HOT

union

union

ing, hot water from the grate enters at the top of the storage tank. Exiting from the bottom of the tank, it recirculates through the grate. This cycle operates by natural heat convection; that is, as water heats, it expands and, like air, becomes less dense and rises. The hot water storage tank must, therefore, be placed higher than the outlet from the heating grate. For water to thermosiphon effectively, either place the storage tank directly above the fireplace or locate it no more than two feet away horizontally for each foot of vertical rise.

Water drawn for domestic use is taken from the upper or hottest level of the tank. Water from an outside source enters at a lower level, replacing any water withdrawn from the system. Because hot water is being removed and then replaced with incoming cold water, this is called an **open** system.

When little water is drawn from the system and when the fire has burned hotly for an extended period of time, water in this system will likely exceed the boiling point, producing steam. As steam pressure builds, an explosion can occur, unless a pressure relief valve has been provided.

All commercial water heaters are equipped with relief valves. If you do not install a commercial tank, you will most certainly have to use such a valve on the storage tank you do select. This valve operates on the fail-safe principle; that is, when the valve fails to work, the system safely opens, allowing the release of steam pressure. A setting of the valve for 30 pounds-per-square-inch is sufficient, for the operating temperature will seldom if ever exceed boiling temperature or a pressure of 12-20 psi. Another possible hazard of this system is that, since a thermostat cannot be installed, it is never known just how hot water in the system has become until its use at the tap. This poses little problem for cognizant adults, but it can be a hazard for children and the unwary.

Even a pressure relief valve will not prevent explosion if air, trapped in a water line at a low point in the system, prevents natural circulation. This can occur if pipe is not laid uniformly in the direction of the water's flow. Any loops or reverses in vertical direction, either upward or downward, will form places in the pipe line for the possible accumulation of air, which can eventually interrupt the continuous flow of water

A check valve is another device essential to the effective operation of this heating system. It is a simple, one-way valve that prevents water from flowing in a direction opposite to that in which it is intended to flow. Without this check valve, for example, water may siphon from the tank back toward the cooler grate after the fire is extinguished. A check valve positioned at the inlet to the fireplace grate and one at the outlet will also produce a pumping action, which will promote an even stronger natural flow. As the fire's heat increases, an intermittant surging of heated water, much like that in a coffee percolator, alternately opens and closes these valves. There are a wide variety of check valves commercially available, but we have found that the "swing" check valve offers the least resistance to slow moving water. This valve consists of a hinged arm that opens to permit the circulation of water in a forward direction only.

The pipe grate is an excellent device for use in low volume systems where hot water is stored and only occasionally used. During winter when the fireplace is in constant use, it should provide most of the hot water a family will need without the use of other fuel. However, this grate does not have the heating capacity to supply large amounts of hot water for constant use in situations such as that required for home space heating. In this case, a device with a larger heating capacity is needed.

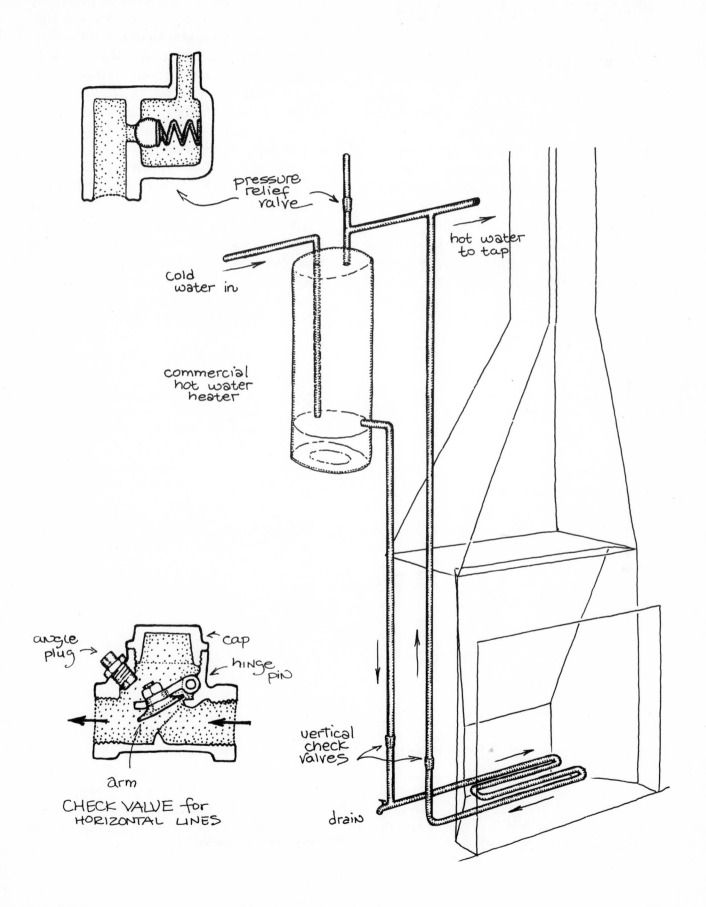

pressure relief valve

cold water in

commercial hot water heater

hot water to tap

angle plug

cap

hinge pin

arm

CHECK VALVE for HORIZONTAL LINES

vertical check valves

drain

Water Jackets

To rapidly acquire large quantities of hot water, we have experimented with a fireplace water jacket of hollow steel which can be fitted into the firebox, either across the fireback wall or flanking the firebox. Water flowing inside the jacket absorbs heat from the fire and passes from the jacket at its highest point into pipes carrying the heated water through a circulating system.

The lone manufacturer of fireplace water jackets in this country charges nearly $1,000. for a unit that, from our point of view, is unsuitable. Its firebox is 28 inches deep — overly large by comparison with the 18-inch depth we prefer to use. Once again, we feel inclined to state that firebox proportions which reflect the radiant heat from an open fire need not be sacrificed just to heat water. Another design flaw of this commercial jacket is that, once it is installed in masonry, there is no possibility that it can be removed if repair should ever become necessary — short of demolishing the entire fireplace.

The water jackets we have presented here are designed to be adapted to operate in conjunction with a masonry firebox. They must be carefully welded to seal all leaks.

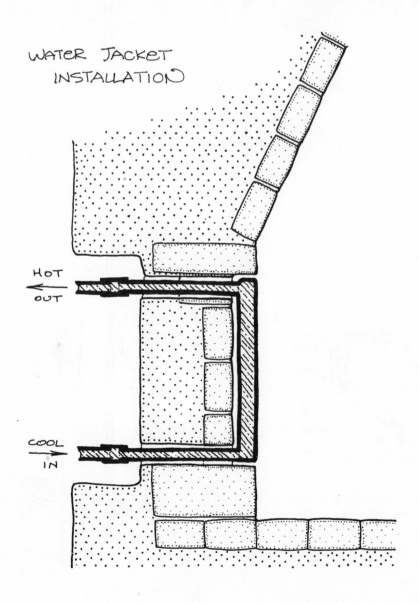

WATER JACKET
INSTALLATION

HOT
OUT

COOL
IN

Test the watertightness of the jacket you build before its installation. Even the smallest hole will leak water once pressure in the system mounts. As recommended for other metal fireplace parts, we suggest the use of no less than 3/16-inch plate steel for this project. These jackets are removable after installation so that, when necessary, they can easily be repaired at any time.

For jacket installation, lay the first course of firebrick to create a platform 4-1/2 inches high and wide enough to carry both the water jacket and a firebrick wall behind it. Shim the jacket to raise it 3/8-inch to allow for heat expansion. In the back wall, leave plenty of room to allow for expansion around inlet and outlet pipes where they go through the masonry. Once you have built firebox walls to the top of the jacket, brick may be corbelled out to become flush with the front of the jacket. The rest of the wall is continued upward from this point in the usual manner.

In the back of the fireplace, leave access to the couplings so that they may be attached and detached when necessary. The owner-built water jacket in the accompanying photograph is fitted with an optional jamb on which doors may be hung. This jamb, as pictured, was made of curved pipe, rather than with flat iron, so that it could more easily be removed. When building over the arched opening, use the pipe as a form but be sure the masonry is, in the final analysis, self-supporting in case the jamb and the jacket ever need removal.

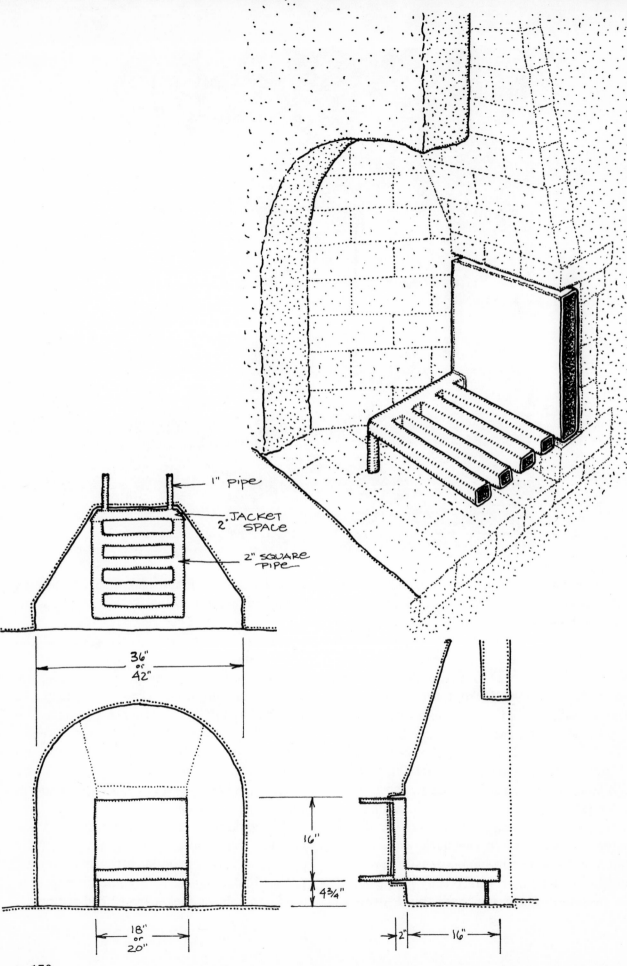

1" PIPE

2" JACKET SPACE

2" SQUARE PIPE

36"
or
42"

18"
or
20"

16"

4¾"

2"

16"

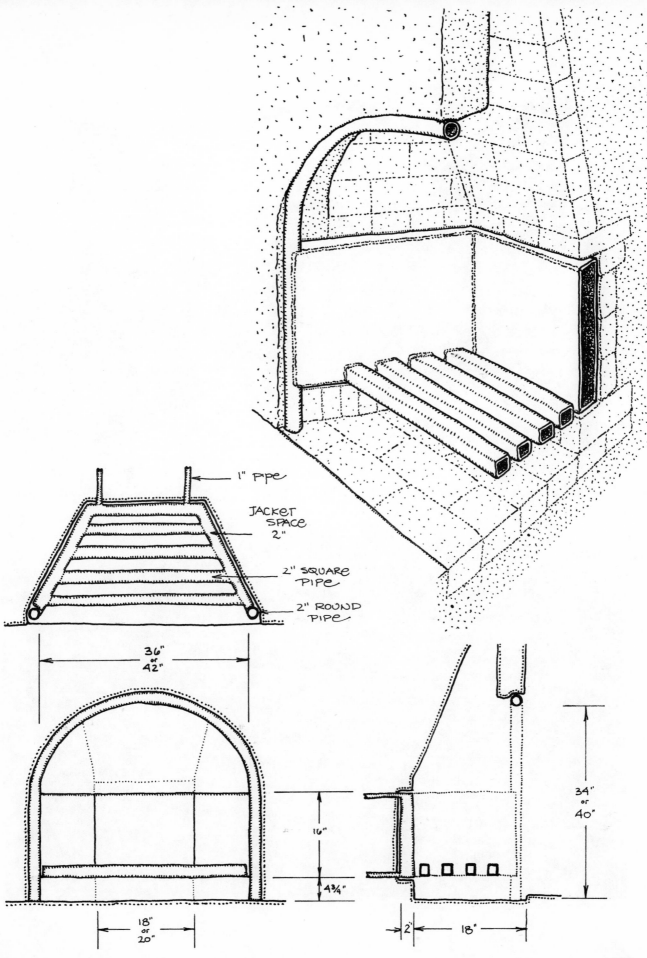

1" pipe

JACKET
SPACE
2"

2" SQUARE
PIPE

2" ROUND
PIPE

36"
or
42"

16"

4¾"

18"
or
20"

2"

18"

34"
or
40"

151

Hot Water Room Heating

The fireplace water jacket makes possible the use of hot water for home heating, for the fire's abundant heat is transported by water to rooms remote from the fireplace. Registers located about perimeter walls radiate the water's heat into rooms. Commercially available, these registers consist of a grill work of square aluminum collars — or fins — which surround a 3/4-inch copper hot-water conducting pipe. These fins are square in shape, instead of round, in order to provide a third more heat-radiating surface area.

Although this type of tubular heating device generally emits radiant heat, it can be enclosed so that air, in contact with the metal fins, will be heated by conduction and will be convected into the living space. On some commercial units, radiant heat or convected heating can be selected by simply regulating a baffle which operates outlet vents.

There are numerous means by which hot water can be transported from the water jacket to floor registers. We are partial to one particular design because it also combines with a solar collector. Instead of using a commercially manufactured water heater for hot water storage, we prefer to use Steve Baer's "breadbox" solar collector. This unit consists simply of a water tank in an insulated box with an insulated door that swings shut at night and on cloudy days. Glass or plastic covers the tank, which is fully exposed to the sun, and forms a heat-retaining chamber. This is by far the simplest, lest costly, and easiest to build of the solar collectors. Complete plans for this design may be obtained from Steve at Zomeworks, Box 712, Albuquerque, New Mexico.

From the jacket, water rises directly to the collector, entering at the top. From the collector, it descends to floor registers, where its heat dissipates into the room. The cooled water then flows back into the water jacket for re-heating. This is known as a **closed loop** system since the same water continuously flows through the circuit, never to be withdrawn. Besides retaining its heat better than an open system, the closed loop system is less corrosive of the steel jacket because no rust-producing oxygen is introduced.

The greater heat capacity of a water jacket can result in a rapid rise in the internal pressure of this heating system. Even before its boiling point is reached, water expands by 5 percent of its volume when heated from 32 to 212 degrees Farenheit. In order to accomodate this expansion, an extra tank must be installed at the highest point in the system. This compression tank is partially filled with pressurized air. As water expands, air compresses and acts as a cushion so that internal pressure rises at a less rapid rate. The size of the tank required for this depends, of course, upon the volume of water in the system.

In an open system, internal pressure is released every time a tap is turned on, minimizing the danger of excess pressure. An expansion tank, however, should be used even on an open system if there will be extended periods of time when domestic hot water is not drawn or when high temperatures, such as those produced in a water jacket, are to be reached.

As in the previously mentioned system, water will continuously flow around the loop as long as a fire heats water in the jacket. If you wish to burn a fire without supplying hot water to perimeter registers, a bypass must be installed so that heated water will circulate only from the jacket to the tank and then directly back to the jacket again. When you wish to heat with stored hot water while a fire is not burning, since the fire's driving force is not present a pump must be used. This pump should be installed, as illustrated, on a bypass check valve. In this way, the pump need only be used when necessary.

One additional elaboration on this closed system allows it to be used for domestic hot water supply. This is accomplished by running a loop of water pipe through the storage tank, an arrangement that is, in effect, another type of heat exchanger. Water in the loop will be heated by water in the storage tank. From this point, it can go directly to household taps. Thus the complete water heating needs for the home are provided.

As with most of the other systems we have outlined, heating water in a fireplace can be traced to antiquity. We found it interesting to note that in 60 AD, a Roman, Seneca the Younger, wrote in a book he called **Quaestione Naturales** that, "Vessels are manufactured, in the interior of which are mounted tubes of very thin copper, which wind round and round. The water contained therein surrounds the fire and has sufficient space so that it can heat itself. It enters cold, comes out boiling, and does not loose its heat through evaporation because it is enclosed."

154

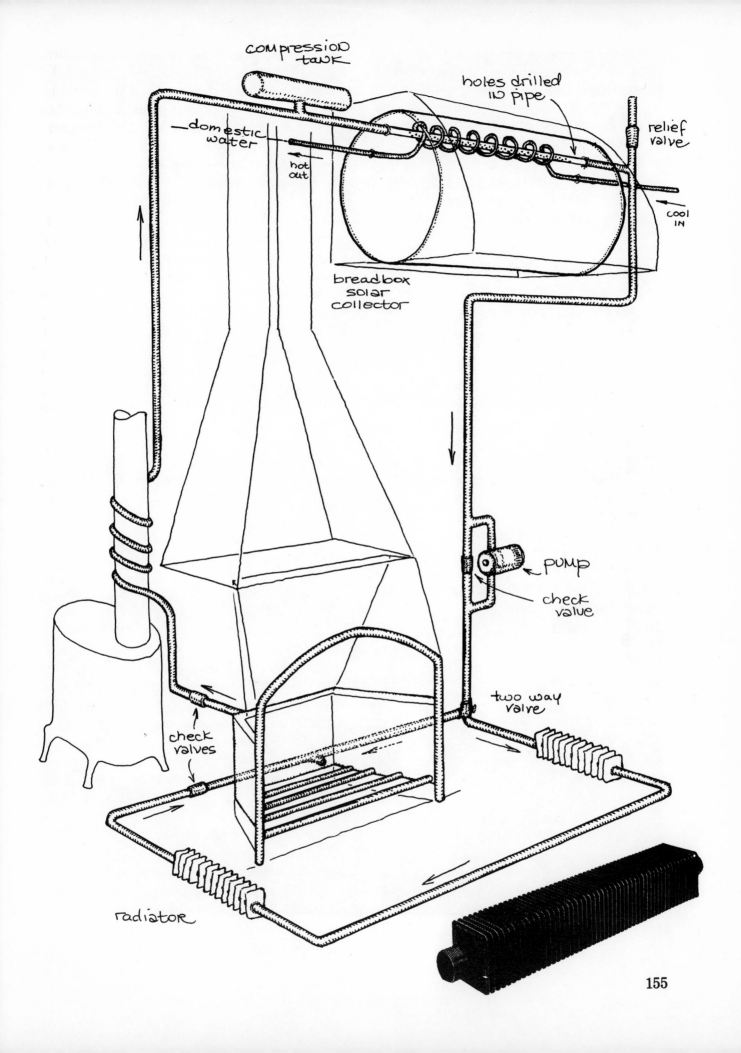

compression
tank

holes drilled
in pipe

relief
valve

domestic
water

hot
out

cool
in

breadbox
solar
collector

PUMP

check
valve

two way
valve

check
valves

radiator

Multi-opening Fireplaces

When tracing its development, we saw that in its beginning the fireplace was simply an open circle of fire. In time, it became a cavernous firebox. With Rumford's innovations, the fire re-emerged into the living area. The next evlutionary step is, logically, to eliminate firebox sides and even the fireback of the fireplace, once again totally exposing the fire to the living space. Although this latter idea is appealing on its surface, the reality is that most fireplaces, built with this premise in mind, work unsatisfactorily. Ironically, such fireplace alterations yield less heat and give a more restricted view of the fire than those open only in front. Futhermore, they require a larger flue area, which results in drawing more room air up the chimney.

The reason these fireplaces are ineffectual is that they are designed on a basis which differs markedly from that of Rumford's. The floor of the multi-opening firebox is rectangular in shape. A hood is positioned over it, with its flue outlet in the center. This hood is supported by masonry or by metal posts, whose placement depends upon which sides of the firebox are to remain open. Being of versatile design, the firebox can be opened on two opposite or two adjoining sides, on three sides, or all around. Unfortunately, for this design to draw well, the lintel must be lowered, with the result that much heat escapes up the chimney and a view of the fire is restricted.

This system, by necessity requires the use of a large, deep firebox with no slanting walls which can reflect heat out-

ward. The fire must be laid at the center of the firebox floor, strictly away from its outer edges. It would seem that this heat system was devised more to withhold heat than to release it.

One may then legitimately question whether there is any practical way to build a multi-opening firebox. We have found there is if you start with the firebox, whose construction we have previously recommended, and if you systematically eliminate unnecessary parts of the box. This must be done without drastically altering those parts which must remain. The lintel must be left intact, box depth should be shallow, and the throat has to be narrow and well forward. If radically altered, heat output will be sacrificed and

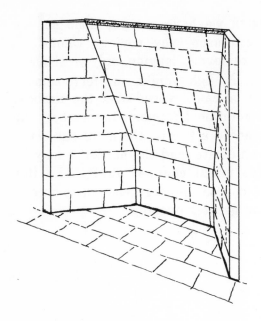

nothing will be gained by the procedure.

To begin eliminating parts of the firebox, cut back the covings. A fireplace, in which this was successfully done, is shown here. The lower sides were not built, and the upper portion of the firebox was gradually cantilevered to support the lintel and the throat. This cantilevered design dispenses with the necessity to use metal support posts, which are unattractive and block one's view of the fire. This modified firebox will radiate slightly more heat than one with full covings. Although it reacts temperamentally when a fire is first lit, it draws well once the chimney is hot. Occasionally, it will smoke when a breeze from an opening blows across the fire.

Although we have not yet done so, we see little reason why covings cannot be entirely removed, leaving only a slanting fireback. A lightweight or ferro-cement hood can be cantilevered over the firebox, without additional support. Remember, the more exposed a fire is, the more subject it is to room drafts, and the harder it may be to induce initial chimney draft. The flue must, of course, be large enough to accomodate the greater opening.

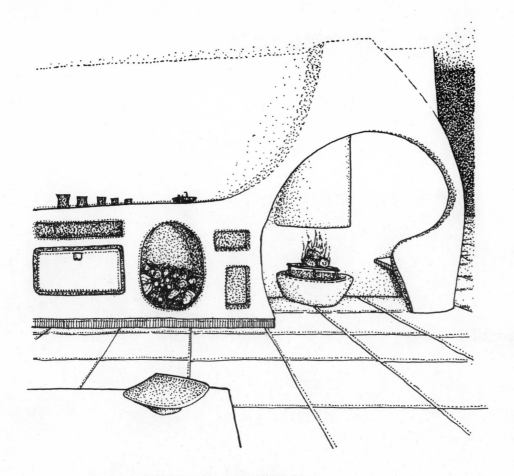

Houses today are less drafty than they must, originally, have been when the fire-circle was first used. This multi-opening fireplace design, with only a hood suspended over the fire, remains however of questionable merit. Such an arrangement is subject to interference from drafts caused merely by the normal activity of passers-by. Nevertheless, we include a free-standing, hooded design for the adventurous who will wish to build a novel device. But we offer one final caution: Build a hood that may be adjusted up and down. This is necessary in order to experimentally determine the height at which the hood will induce proper fireplaced draft.

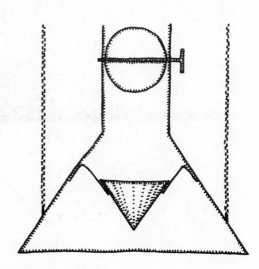

Rotating Fireplace

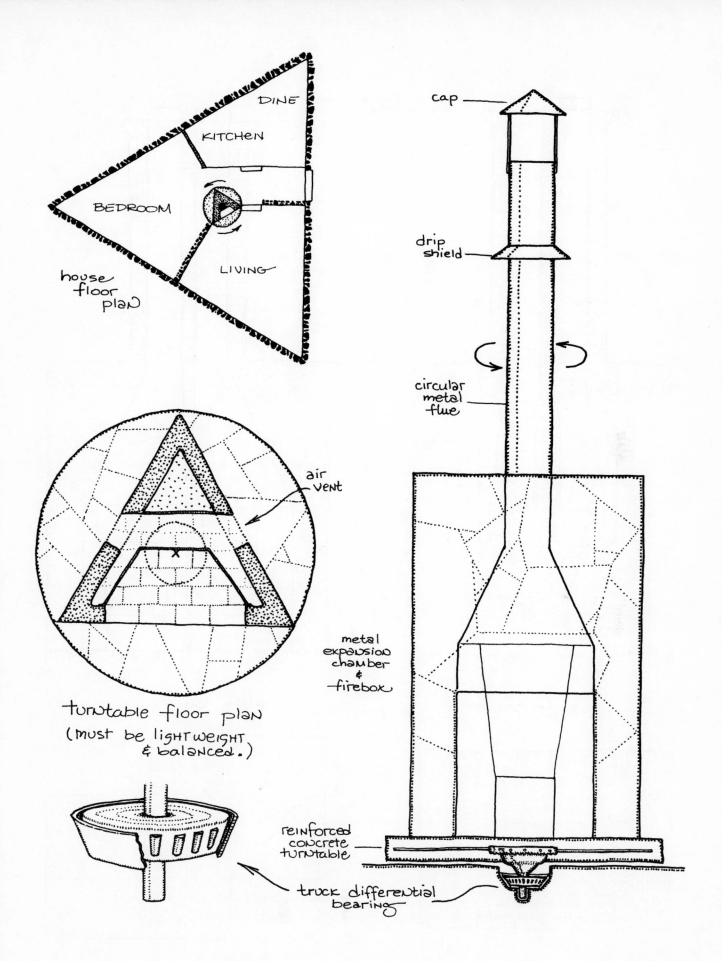

DINE

KITCHEN

BEDROOM

LIVING

house floor plan

cap

drip shield

circular metal flue

air vent

turntable floor plan
(must be lightweight & balanced.)

metal expansion chamber & firebox

reinforced concrete turntable

truck differential bearing

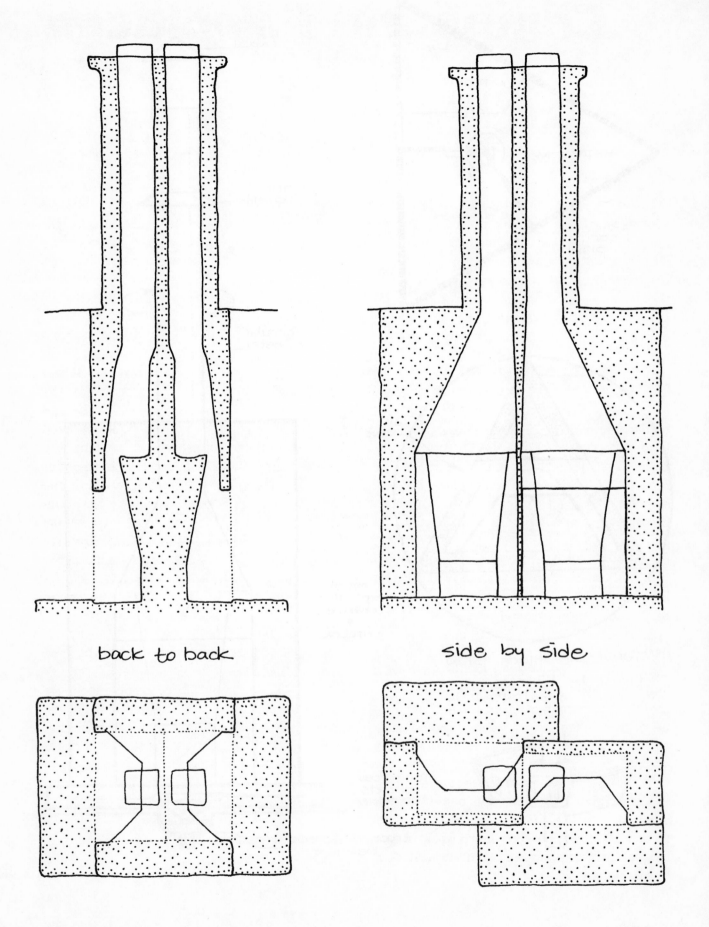

back to back   side by side

Compound Fireplaces

If you wish to have several fireplaces located in different rooms of the house, it is most practical to combine them into a single structure. To build two, separate fireplaces and two chimneys will take twice the time and materials required to build two fireplaces in a single structure, using only a third more labor and material. There are, of course, disadvantages to this; mainly, that for the savings you will realize, you will sacrifice some flexibility of design, and placement of the two fireplaces will necessarily be limited. Also, the additional investment cannot be postponed to a later time; it must be made at once. The reason for this is that a fireplace is built sequentially from the ground up, and both fireboxes in a combination unit must be completed before a chimney for the unit can be built.

Within these limits, there is considerable leeway for arrangement of the two fireplaces. If they are placed on the same level of the house, they may be built back-to-back, creating a square, compact shape. Or they may be arranged side-by-side for a long narrower form that will divide two rooms. The two fireplaces do not need to be at the same height; one may be in a room on the ground floor and the other in a second floor space.

To build several fireplaces requires more space than to build a single one. You can expect a second unit built on the same floor to add about 75 percent more area to the base of this combination structure. It is a challenge to arrange two fireplaces to fit next to one another in an efficient way. To succeed requires that you are aware of the space needed by each fireplace for its entire length. Because they adapt at floor level does not necessarily mean that they will fit at smokeshelf level.

If the two fireplaces are located above one another on two different levels, you must decide how you will route the flue of the lower one around the firebox of the upper one. If this is done correctly, the size of the base and the masonry below need not be radically increased to support the upper unit. Build the expansion chamber and flue of the lower fireplace to tilt to one side within the 8-foot room height customarily found in a standard room. A common practice is to build the upper fireplace opening about 6 inches narrower than the lower one, allowing space to one side for the passage of the flue from the lower fireplace. Many variations are possible, such as adding a wood box to the fireplace below to create additional, weight-bearing masonry for the upper fireplace.

Even if there is little room on the upper level of the house for a full-sized fireplace, there may be a space to build a small one. Perhaps only 24 inches wide, this diminutive fireplace can provide a cherry, cozy atmosphere in den or sleeping quarters. You will find that even a fireplace of this size will give heat sufficient to warm a space of reasonable size.

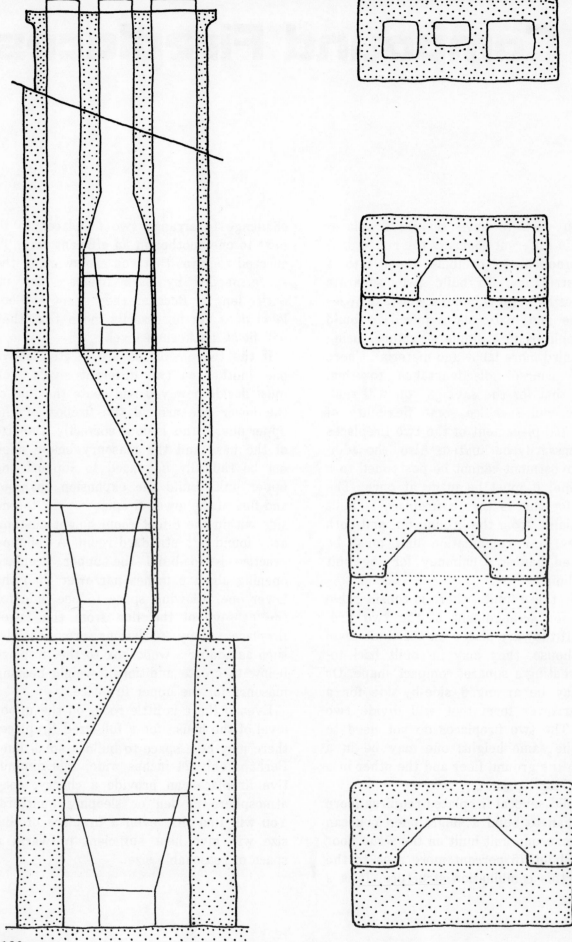

UPPER LEVEL FIREPLACES

Try to visualize where flue from lower fireplace is located.

Woodstove Chimneys

When building a fireplace, it is advisable to include as many flues as you ever expect to need. Even if you have no immediate use for a woodstove in an adjoining room, include a flue outlet for one anyway. Its additional expense is slight, but its inclusion gives greater flexibility to your heating system. The woodstove is the most efficient wood heating facility yet devised, and although it lacks the charm of the fireplace, it may be a wise choice as a primary source of heat for the home.

To plan a woodstove-and-fireplace unit, a number of factors must be considered. It is necessary to position them to get the maximum heating benefit from each. Quality woodstoves and fireplaces are objects of beauty and should be seen separately for their best appreciation. Placed side by side, these two objects compete for attention and are redundant in function. They should, therefore, be placed in a complementary position, perhaps on opposite sides of the masonry structure, in different rooms, or even on different levels of a house. Each house design will suggest the proper configuration for these devices.

Separate wood burning facilities must have separate flues in order to function properly. Once the relative positions of the woodstove and fireplace have been determined, it is necessary to plan how the various flues will fit into the chimney structure. It takes considerable planning to choose the best arrangement of flues so that the chimney will be as compact as possible when it passes through the roof.

A woodstove flue is far simpler than a fireplace flue. Since most of the vents, heat reclaimers, dampers, etc., are built into the woodstove itself, the flue functions only to provide an exit for smoke. However simple it is, the flue must still be designed for maximum efficiency and convenience. A woodstove is an enclosed system, so its flue draw is rarely a problem. The only requirement is that its cross sectional area must be at least the same size as the metal pipe which connects stove to masonry.

If draft is satisfactory, then the major problem will be how to maintain a clean flue. A woodstove operates at a much lower combustion rate than a fireplace; its smoke rises more slowly up the chimney flue and contains less heat. As a result, creosote build-up becomes both a concern and an inconvenience. This is especially true of airtight stoves. When in combination with an improperly designed chimney, these stoves often exhibit clogged flues and a flow of gummy tars from fittings.

The three things required from a successfully operating woodstove chimney are that it keep rain out, maintain chimney heat, and contain a clean-out space in which to collect soot and creosote. To make a woodstove flue, first construct the soot cleanout chamber and its door. Making this chamber is similar to building the ash clean-out for a fireplace. It may be positioned anywhere beneath the stove pipe connection, which is commonly called a thimble. This chamber collects soot and chunks of creosote that build up and drop down from flue walls. Without this compartment below the thimble, debris can collect at the elbow formed by the thimble and flue where it can catch fire.

The floor of the clean out chamber should slope slightly away from its door, so that when it is opened, soot collected against the door will not spill into the room. The clean out may be located either inside or outside the house. Seal its opening with an 8 x 8 or a 8 x 12-inch door. This lower chamber should be air-tight so that the chimney above will draw well. It should not therefore, be tied in with the fireplace ash pit. The passage from soot chamber to

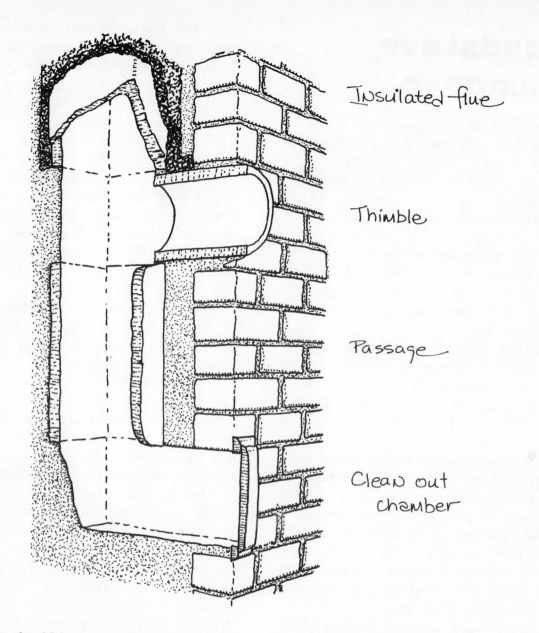

Insulated flue

Thimble

Passage

Clean out chamber

chimney should be smooth and straight, allowing debris to drop directly to the clean-out chamber. Although it is wise to use an 8-inch-square flue liner for this passage, smoothly parged brick will work equally well. For an unobstructed drop to the clean-out chamber, it is advisable to position the soot chamber directly below the thimble. This chamber must sometimes be offset in the chimney, however, so that the wood-stove will not block its access.

The woodstove is connected to the masonry chimney by a metal pipe which fits into the thimble. Different stoves require varying flue size. Install the maximum size of pipe and thimble you ever anticipate needing. Metal reducers can be used if the opening is too large. The thimble connects directly with the flue and soot dump, forming a tee-shape. From this point, the flue should rise as vertically as possible. However, angles may be necessary for the compact arrangement of chimney flues. Closely positioned flues have the added advantage of sharing heat mutually. When building angles and bends, make certain the change in direction is not so abrupt that it inhibits draft, accumulates soot, or makes cleaning difficult.

The hotter the flue, the better it will draw. Although draft itself is rarely a problem, a hot flue discourages the condensation of creosote on flue walls. It is, therefore, a distinct advantage to insulate the flue liner from the rest of the masonry to prevent the dissipation of heat. The insulating material should be rigid to support the flue liner and to prevent its loss through cracks which sometimes develop in ceramic linings. For this, we recommend a mixture of Portland cement and vermiculite or perlite. These are mineral materials which have been heat-treated in order for them to expand into a lightweight aggregate. A mixture of water and 6-parts aggregate to 1-part cement forms a concrete that has adequate strength and improved insulating properties. Apply this concrete around the flue liner to a thickness of about 2 inches. At the top of the chimney, protect this insulating layer from exposure to rainwater with a layer of conventional mortar.

Even a well insulated flue should be cleaned at least once a year. With a regular schedule for cleaning, an owner can do the work, using a long-handled wire brush made specifically for this purpose.

Flues built side-by-side should be separated by a fill of at least 2 inches of solid masonry material. This precaution insures that there will be no smoke leaks between the two if cracking occurs.

A chimney cap over a woodstove flue is essential, for rainwater can cause havoc a woodstove system by its rusting of metal parts. Also, water running down the flue liner will cool it and cause greater creosote build-up; it also carries soot down the flue and through the soot door, staining masonry.

Fireplace Cooking

There was a time when cooking constituted a primary function of the home fireplace. In Colonial America, every fireplace held a cast iron cooking pot to heat water or simmer a stew. A brick oven, built into the masonry, was well known for its even heat and its consistent results. Over the years with the popularization of the wood cookstove and, later, with its gas and electric counterparts, the fireplace as a cooking facility gradually faded. The patio barbecue is about the only remnant of fireplace cooking. This method of food preparation requires that the cook have a knack for this work, which is something developed with experience. We are including ideas for several fireplace cooking accessories, for those of you who may wish to revive this art in your home.

Pot hangers may be installed inside the firebox to position a cooking pot directly

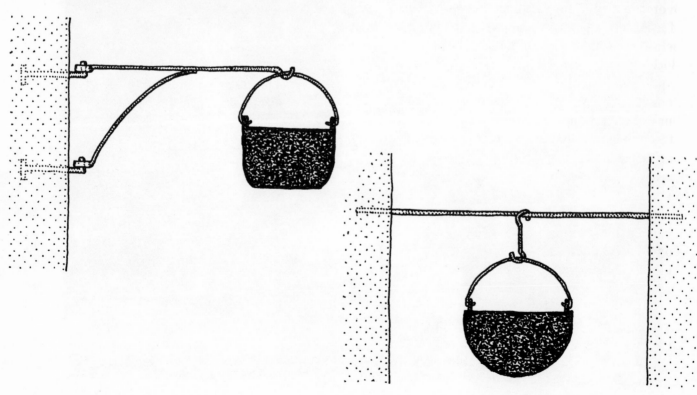

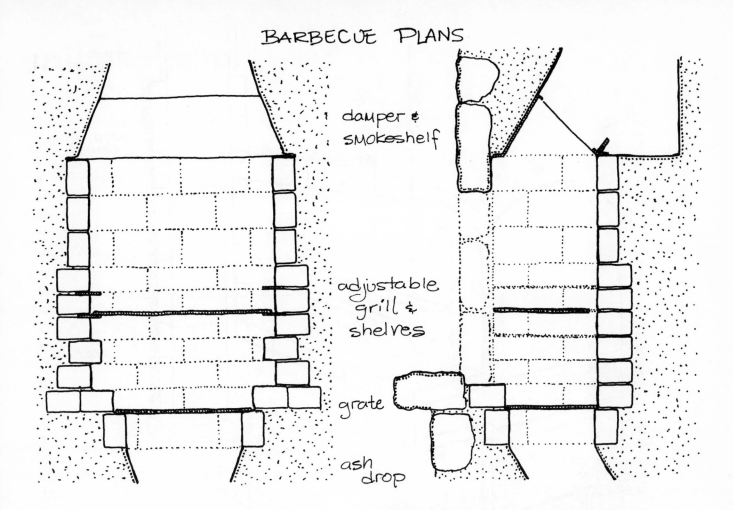

damper & smokeshelf

adjustable grill & shelves

grate

ash drop

over the fire. The simplest device consists of a metal rod which spans the firebox just below the throat, like a closet clothes pole. Both ends are embedded in masonry or are welded to the sides of a metal firebox. A pot hook hangs from this rod. A more elaborate but convenient pot hanger is a swinging arm attached to the firebox wall. It must be well anchored in masonry to support the arm and its heavy pot as they swing in and out of the fireplace.

By putting a metal grill over coals in a fireplace, campfire style cooking can be done. A refinement of this method is to build a separate barbecuing space in the fireplace structure. This recess should be at a convenient working height and be designed to retain its heat for efficient cooking. The front opening should be only 2 feet square and contain an adjustable rack for various grill heights.

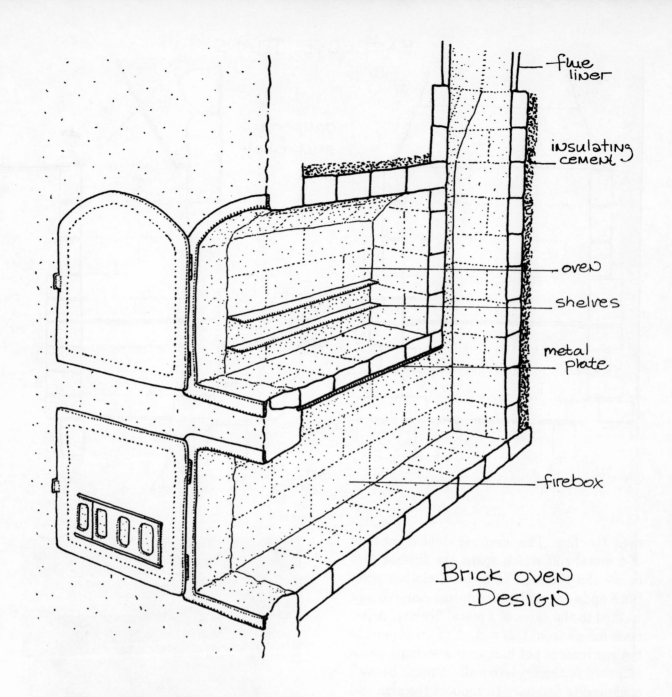

flue
liner

insulating
cement

oven

shelves

metal
plate

firebox

Brick oven
DESIGN

The brick oven is another cooking facility that can be built into the fireplace structure. This device consists of a brick-lined container over a fire chamber. Its oven is heated by the fire and by rising flue gases, which pass around it on several sides. Once its brick heats, the oven will maintain a constant temperature for long periods — an optimal condition for baking bread and casseroles.

Both the oven and the firechamber require doors. These may be bought from a manufacturer of metal doors or may be custom-made. To regulate the rate of combustion, the fire chamber door should have an adjustable air vent. The oven door must fit tightly to prevent heat escape. A thermometer and even a glass window for observing the cooking food may be built into it. There was a time when the brick oven was considered a necessity in every well equipped kitchen.

174

It is helpful to have a firewood storage compartment built into the fireplace masonry. This is a safer place to store firewood than on the hearth, which is vulnerable to flying sparks from the fire. A woodbox will increase the floor area of the fireplace and require additional time and materials to build, but if you decide these problems are worth its convenience, make the firebox large enough to hold full-sized logs. Its floor should be smooth so that debris can easily be swept from it. The twigs, sawdust, and dried leaves that inevitably collect there can be a fire hazard if the woodbox wall should get excessively hot.

If your fireplace adjoins an exterior wall of the house, the woodbox may have a door which allows you to lead it directly from the woodpile outside, avoiding much effort and mess. Even if this arrangement is not possible, it may still be desirable to provide a firewood access door in a wall near the fireplace.

FIRESPACES

People in this country are becoming dependent upon electric power in almost every aspect of their lives. In some homes, you cannot brush your teeth or open a can of food without using electricity. This dependancy is actively encouraged by power companies, who stand to profit by creating an "electric habit" in the consumer public and by encouraging wasteful energy consumption through lower rates given to high volume users. Other beneficiaries of these wasteful practices are the coal and oil companies, who sell their raw material for electric power generation, and the makers of those myriad electrical devices we all use indiscriminantly.

In his book, **The Poverty of Power,** Barry Commoner points out that it is more efficient to burn fuel directly in the home than to produce electrical energy at a distant source, only to lose two-thirds of it from transmission lines to the home. Even after it reaches the home, electricity used for heating is inefficient and expensive. Paul

Howell, an owner-builder of Morrisville, NY, has calculated the energy needed to heat homes having varying degrees of insulation and using electric, oil, or wood energy. As you can see by Howell's table, electric heat is much more expensive and consumes twice the energy of wood heat.

The owner-builder seeking freedom from dependance on electricity usage will find it difficult to achieve. The Uniform Building Code, for instance, compels a builder to install a thermostatically controlled heating system which can, at any time, distribute 70-degree heat throughout the home. Owner-builders who choose to heat with wood fail to comply with this code restriction, despite the advantage and the commonsense of wood heat use.

With this fair warning that our suggestions may not be code approved, we arrive at the place in this book where we will attempt to integrate all the elements of efficient fireplace heating previously dis-

ANNUAL FUEL CONSUMPTION (Million BTU/yr) and COST
Northern U.S. Winter: Ave. Temp. 30° F., Temp. diff. 40° F.

House Heating	Electric at 30% Efficiency			Oil Burner at 80% Efficiency			Wood at 60% efficiency		
Insulation	mBTU used	1000 KWH	cost at 2c/KWH	mBTU used	gal.	cost at 40c/gal	mBTU used	full cords	cost at $60/cord
Shoddy	376	33	$660	141	1000	$400	188	7.5	$450
Standard	268	23.6	472	101	720	290	134	5.4	325
Snug									
Continuous	103	9.1	182	39	280	112	52	2.1	126
Earth Nights	62	5.5	110	23	165	66	31	1.25	75

cussed with the additional benefits of dwelling space built with adequate insulation, effective air circulation, solar orientation, and thermal mass heat storage. This synthesis of these components creates what is, to us, a highly efficient, esthetically pleasing household heating system: the **firespace.**

To develop this concept of the firespace, look again at Howell's energy-use table. In the last column, he compares the energy needed to continuously heat a snugly insulated house with that needed to heat a house which receives nighttime warmth radiating from a masonry floor and the earth below it; a system Howell calls "earth nights." Both floor and earth act as a thermal mass, storing heat from sun and fireplace during the day and releasing it at night. Such back-up heat storage may save half the home heating bill.

In the following text, we will illustrate a series of firespace designs, from the simplest to the more elaborate. Owner-builders may then choose that system which best suits their heating needs, economy, and climate.

The simplest firespace design is a small, compact house with a centrally located fireplace-and-stove heating core. Wall and ceiling insulation is of primary importance in this initial design. Not only necessary for household comfort, adequate insulation is critical to the efficient use of the fireplace; e.g. an inadequately insulated house requires the use of more fuel to maintain a warm interior temperature than a well insulated house. In summer, a poorly insulated house requires additional energy to maintain a cool, comfortable interior environment. The greatest return from any capital investment in house building accrues from the application of adequate thermal insulation.

Insulation prevents moisture condensation on cold, interior surfaces and floor drafts produced by the convective air currents generated by temperature differences on wall surfaces. Household air leaks must be located and weather-stripped or caulked. Insulated curtains or panels should cover large window areas at night and occasionally on cold, cloudy winter days. These practices will dramatically reduce general heat loss.

The exterior walls of this first firespace design should be built to accomodate 6 inches of insulation. Ceilings should be filled with twice this amount, and masonry floors should be circumscribed with perimeter insulation. In northern climates, to further minimize heat loss all windows should be double glazed and doors carefully weather-stripped.

Another table prepared by Howell compares heat loss from the house "shoddily" built with a house meeting the minimum property standards established by FHA. Note that these structures require, respectively, 3.6-times and 2.6-times more energy consumption than that of the snug house.

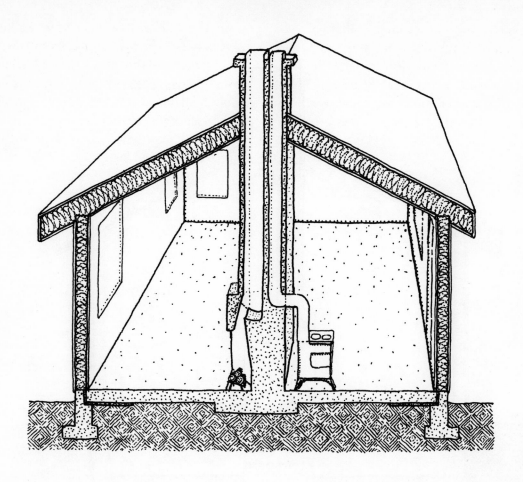

HEAT LOSS: BTU/hr. at 80 degrees temperature difference

	Area: sq. ft.	SHODDY		STANDARD		SNUG	
		R	BTU/hr	R	BTU/hr	R	BTU/hr
Ceiling	1000	6	13300	20	4000	40	2000
Walls	860	6	11500	12	5800	20	3400
Windows	100	1	8000	1	8000	2	4000
Floor	1000	edge	8000	edge	8000	10	2000
Air infiltration			11000		11000		2800
TOTAL HEAT LOSS			51800		36800		14200

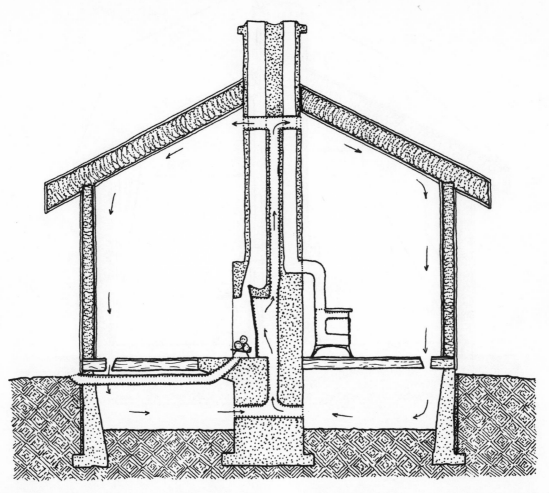

Although, energy-wise, this first firespace design is superior to the average dwelling, it has some features that may nevertheless be unsatisfactory. For instance, much room heat is drawn up the fireplace flue, while the remainder tends to accumulate at ceiling level. In our second firespace design, a duct brings in outside air for fireplace combustion, thereby preventing a depletion of the warm air supply.

A passive system of circulating air can raise fireplace efficiency considerably. In this scheme, the fireplace is equipped with a hot-air circulating chamber. As air in this compartment is heated, it expands and rises to the ceiling. As it begins to cool, it flows down walls to floor slots along perimeter walls. Once it enters these slots, it travels through an insulated basement or crawl space from whence it is drawn back into the recovery chamber at the base of the fireplace. Air movement, in other words, follows a path of circulation through the central masonry core, across the ceiling, down exterior walls, and through a basement or crawl space — returning again to the fireplace. It does not pass, as a floor draft, across the living zone.

There is another important principle in operation here. While surface temperatures fluctuate, subterranean temperature at the 8-foot level is almost constant at 58-degrees. Earth, therefore, tends to modify either hotter or colder air in its proximity. Household temperature extremes are thus regulated, particularly when heat sources are dormant. Note the wintertime fuel saving in the first of Howell's charts, when there is no

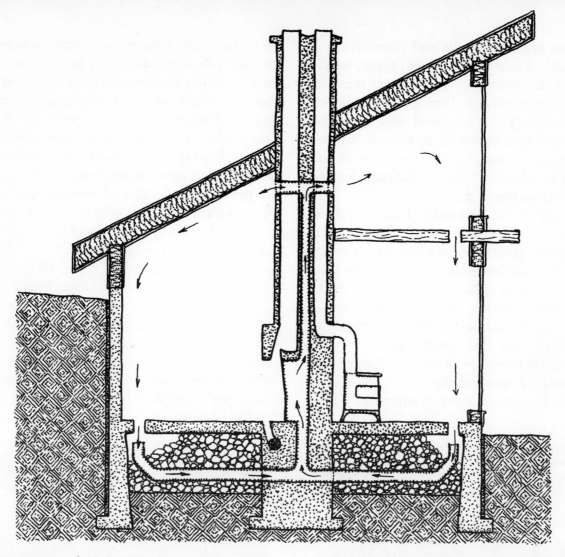

other source of nighttime heat except that held constant by earth temperature. Chill outside air, brought in for fireplace combustion will also be tempered by its passage through this source of constant temperature. The warmer the combustion air, the greater the burning efficiency.

Cooperation with natural forces and knowledge gained through experience can help us to use commonly available resources to satisfy our living needs. We should, therefore, begin to design dwelling space for a wiser use and husbandry of these resources. Wood fuel, building insulation, constant ground temperature, and a passive system of circulating air can work for us in our homes, even to eliminating the necessity for a fuel-fired or electrically-powered back-up heat system.

Wood is essentially stored solar energy. Its burning reverses the photosynthetic process by which it is produced. The heat from its release is comparable, therefore, to the radiant heat from the solar energy that created it. Radiant heat from either of these sources, however, can only be of fleeting advantage if not captured and conserved in some manner. It must be stored for use at times when emanations of heat energy from sun and fire cease.

Our next firespace design expressed our preference for a heating system which operates passively, without electrically powered pumps or fans. In this design, we store heat in a thermal mass, consisting of large bodies of masonry or other similar materials, which absorb heat and re-radiate it long afterward. A masonry fireplace is excellent thermal mass, as are stone walls and floors. So is a gravel-filled basement or crawl space, which adds to the volume of the thermal mass in this particular design. During evening hours and on cloudy days, stored heat may be recovered from this cavity by natural convection brought about by the operation of the fireplace, which acts as an immense suction device when burning.

The structural elements of the fireplace now are: a low-profile earth-bermed north wall, which excludes cold wind; a high south wall, which captures the warmth of the sun; and a sleeping loft, where surplus heat, accumulated during daytime and evening hours, can be maintained through the night by closing a few floor registers.

Our final firespace design synthesizes all presently known techniques for realizing a passive system of thermal efficiency. This self-operative system not only warms a house in winter but cools it in summer. The sun's winter rays penetrate the two layers of plastic which cover a south-facing roof-mounted solar collector and concentrate the sun's infrared rays on a black-painted tank of water. During evenings and on cloudy days, an insulated panel covers the collector tank to prevent the escape of accumulated heat. The storage medium in the tank is water, which is heated by the sun and by circulation through coils in the fireplace and woodstove, or cookstove. It is the source of all domestic hot water and of baseboard room heating.

In summer, the north-sloping roof contributes nighttime cooling to the household. As the white-painted roof surface reflects long-wave radiation to the night sky, its temperature drops, cooling air that moves through passages beneath it. This cooled air then

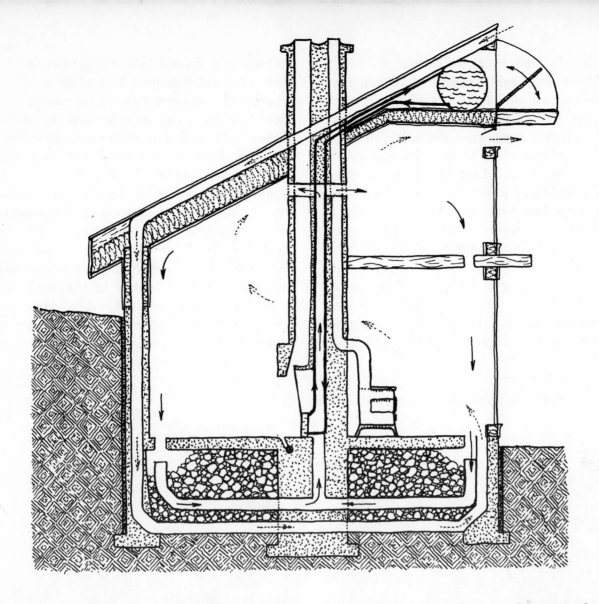

flows into opened wall ducts, down to the crawl space where stored gravel is likewise cooled. Flowing by natural convection across this cavity, cool air enters the house interior through floor registers at the south wall of the building, where it begins to warm and rise, circulating throughout the household to open vents at the peak of the loft. These vents are closed the following morning so that the house will remain relatively cool until daytime incoming shortwave radiation exceeds nighttime outgoing longwave radiation. While the sun is high, its rays are prevented from shining directly into the house by a properly designed roof overhang on the south side of the building and by using few east and west windows.

This last, comprehensive firespace design can be owner-built for nominal cost. However, such a sensible system of heating will not qualify its builder for a government grant or the tax exemption now available to those who will install a costly "approved" (manufactured) solar collector. To get this assistance, an owner-builder would have to install an apparatus of highly technological design, operating at least in part by electricity. A wood-fueled fireplace will not qualify a homeowner for government assistance, no matter how imaginatively conceived or how effectively operative. An example of an approved system is illustrated here for those who may wish to invest in a "active" solar heating system.

Nation-wide concern for dwindling energy reserves and their consequent higher cost have stimulated industry and government to promote "minimum energy dwellings" throughout this country—destined solely for those who can afford to buy this concept of "minimum." The example we have illustrated here was a project sponsored by the federal government and the Southern California Gas Company and financed by a $230,000 government grant. Their goal was to reduce the energy consumption of an averaged-sized tract house of 1200 square feet by 50 percent. Solar energy is the back-up source for this natural gas system which cools and heats this house. Domestic hot water is heated in the same manner.

It is a little known fact that as much energy is expended to heat water for domestic use as is used to heat an entire house in winter. Our alternative prototype not only uses heated water for household heating but for a year-round supply of domestic hot water as well. Pipes connect the fireplace and woodstove to the collector tank, boosting the temperature of solar heated water and circulating it for both house heat and domestic hot water use. We consider water to be the best medium for this collection and heating system, for it has the highest heat-capacity-per-pound of any readily available storage material.

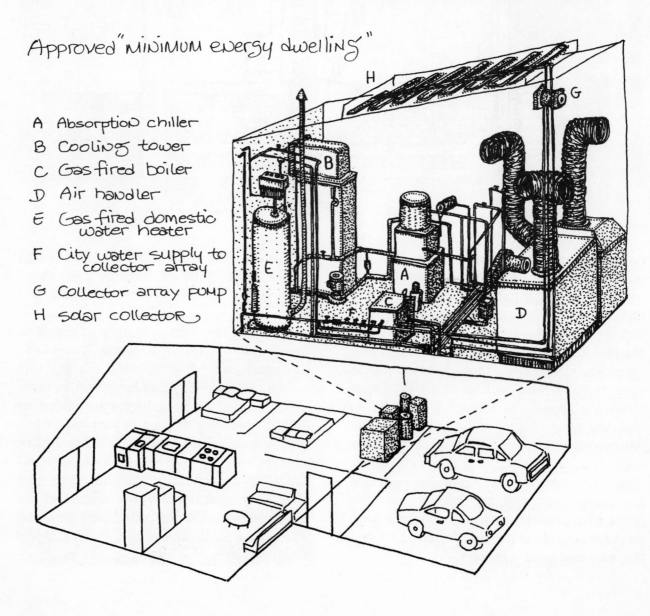

Approved "minimum energy dwelling"

A Absorption chiller
B Cooling tower
C Gas fired boiler
D Air handler
E Gas fired domestic water heater
F City water supply to collector array
G Collector array pump
H Solar collector

The National Bureau of Standards estimates that national energy needs double every fourteen years. We can reverse this trend, as Ralph Nader suggests, by changing our lifestyles. It can also be done in part by building a more efficiently designed and more adequately insulated house. Energy savings are inherent in the wood-burning firespace, with its free sources of ground and solar heat. In this system, we have conserved energy by accumulating and storing heat in water and thermal mass and by circulating it by natural air convection for use, particularly, when sources of heat are dormant. It is our hope that this book has shown the owner-builder how to design and build such an efficient home heating facility — the firespace — which can provide beauty and comfort affordable by all.

RELATED READING

Fireplace Books

The Lost Art of Building a Good Fireplace, Vrest Orton, Yankee Publications, Dublin, N.H., 1969.
>A detailed account of Count Rumford and his fireplaces.

How to Plan and Build Your Fireplace, A Sunset Book, Lane Books, Menlo Park, Calif, 1962.
>Picture book.

Book of Successful Fireplaces, Lyttle & Lyttle, Structures Publishing Co., Farmington, Mi., 1971.
>Picture Book.

Woodstove Books

The Woodburners Encyclopedia, Shelton & Shapiro, Vermont Crossroads Press, Waitsfield, Vt., 1976.
>Excellent, detailed information on woodstoves and how they work.

Heating with Wood, Larry Gay, Garden Way Publishing, Charlotte, Vt., 1974.

Woodburning Stoves, Bob & Carol Ross, Overlook Press, Woodstock, N.Y., 1976.
>Information on modern and classic woodstoves, good chapter on the energy crisis.

Solar Energy Books

The Solar Home Book, Bruce Anderson, Cheshire Books, Harrisville, N.H., 1976.
>Most complete book on the subject to date.

Periodicals

Alternative Sources of Energy, $1.75/issue, Route 2—Box 90A, Milaca, Minn., 56353.

Wood Burning Quarterly & Home Energy Digest, $1.50/issue, 8009 34th Ave., S., Minneapolis, Minn., 55420.

Owner-builder Books

Stone Masonry, Kern, Magers, & Penfeld, Owner-Builder Publications, Oakhurst, Calif, 1976.

The Owner-Built Home, Ken Kern, Chas. Scribner's Sons, N.Y., 1972.

The Owner-Built Homestead, Ken & Barbara Kern, Chas. Scribner's Sons, N.Y., 1977.

The Owner-Builder and the Code, Kern, Kogon, & Thallon, Owner-Builder Publications, Oakhurst, Calif, 1976.

The Healthy House, Ken Kern, Owner-Builder Publications, Oakhurst, Calif, 1978.

Project Credits

front cover — Lynn Walter, mason; Hamlet speculation, Bynum, N.C.

2 — Steve Magers, mason; McLean residence, Pittsboro, N.C.

6 — Ken Kern, mason; North Fork CA

10 — Wayne Trapp, designer; sculpture house near Cleveland, Ohio

17 — Lynn Walters, restorer; Kerney Bynum house, Pittsboro, N.C.

19 — Steve Magers, mason; Marriott residence, Pittsboro, N.C.

20 — Michael Eckerman, mason;felton, Ca.

23 — Billy Mason, mason;Deaton residence; Pittsboro, N.C.

24-26 — 75 year old fireplaces near Chapel Hill, N.C.

27 — Susanna Stewart, owner-builder, Pittsboro, N.C.

28 — Michael Carty, mason; Grumette residence, Pittsboro, N.C.

30 top — Lynn Walters, mason; Hamlet speculation, Bynum, N.C.

bottom — Steve Magers, mason; Ostrom house, Chapel Hill, N.C.

31 — Lynn Walters, mason; Hamlet speculation, Bynum, N.C.

33 — Michael Carty, mason; Pittsboro, N.C.

35 top — Kathy Jones, mason; Hamlet speculation, Bynum, N.C.

bottom — Tom Kenlan, mason; Pittsboro, N.C.

36 — 75 year old fireplace near Chapel Hill, N.C.

37 — Lynn Walters, mason; Hamlet speculation, Bynum, N.C.

38-39 — Bill Goldrick, welder; Pittsboro, N.C.

40 — Richard & Lana Hargrader, owner-builders; Durham, N.C.

41 — Paul Sturges, designer; Stone Ridge, N.Y.

42 — John Sprungman, mason; Manson's Landing, B.C.. Canada

43 — Ernie Milloy, wood seat builder; McLean residence, Pittsboro, N.C.

44 — Ken Kern, designer; North Fork, Calif.

49 — Michael Eckerman, mason; Santa Cruz, Calif.,

50 — Tom Kenlan & Steve Magers, masons; Royal residence, Pittsboro, N.C.

51 — Steve Magers, mason; Pittsboro, N.C.

54 — Steve Magers, mason; Pittsboro, N.C.

59 — Steve Magers & Tom Kenlan, masons; Smith residence, Pittsboro, N.C.

60-78 — Steve Magers & Lynn Walters, masons; Clement residence, Carrboro, N.C.

82 — Lou Penfield, owner-builder; Willoughby Hills, Ohio

83 — Lymance chimney damper; Lousiville, Ky.

84-93 — Steve Magers & Lynn Walters, masons; Clement residence, Carrboro, N.C.

98 left — Bill Goldrick, metal worker; Spalt residence, Pittsboro, N.C.

right — John Sprungman, mason; Mason's Landing, B.C., Canada

100 top — Grimsley Hobbs, owner-builder; Pittsboro, N.C.

bottom — Steve Magers, owner-builder; Pittsboro, N.C.

101 bottom — Steve Magers, Tom & Alice Marriott, masons; Pittsboro, N.C.

102 — Bill Goldrick, metal worker; Spalt residence, Pittsboro, N.C.

103 — Lana & Richard Hargrader, owner-builders; Durham, N.C.

104 — Ken Kern, designer; North Fork, Calif.

106 — John Sprungman, mason; Manson's Landing, B.C., Canada

110-111 — Steve Magers & Joe Kenlan, masons; Doyle residence, Graham, N.C.

112 top — Michael Eckerman, mason; Santa Cruz, Calif.

bottom — Grey residence, Chapel Hill, N.C.

113 — Michael Eckerman, mason; Santa Cruz, Calif.

118-120 — Bill Goldrick, metal worker; Pittsboro, N.C.

121-124 — Steve Magers & Joe Kenlan, masons; Doyle residence, Graham, N.C.

Photography Credits

FRONT COVER—Susanna Stewart
1—Lynn Walters
2—Lynn Walters
4—Michael Eckerman
6—Michael Eckerman
10—Tisa Penfield
17—Lynn Walters
19—Lynn Walters
20—Michael Eckerman
23—Lynn Walters
24—Lynn Walters
25—Bill Marriott
26—Susanna Stewart
27—Susanna Stewart
28—Lynn Walters
30—Lynn Walters
31—Lynn Walters
32—Lou Penfield
33 top—Lynn Walters
    bottom—Steve Magers
35—Lynn Walters
36—Lynn Walters
37—Lynn Walters
38-9—Steve Magers
40—Lana Hargrader
41—Paul Sturges
42—John Sprungman
43—Lynn Walters
44—Michael Eckerman
49—Michael Eckerman
50—Steve Magers
51 top—Michael Eckerman
    bottom—Lynn Walters
53—Lynn Walters
54—Lynn Walters
56—Lynn Walters
59—Lynn Walters
60-78—Lynn Walters
82—Lou Penfield
83—Lymace International
84-93—Lynn Walters
96—Lynn Walters
98 left—Lynn Walters
    right—John Sprungman
99—Lynn Walters
100 top—Lynn Walters
    bottom—Steve Magers

101 bottom—Lynn Walters
102—Lynn Walters
103—Lynn Walters
104—Louis Pavledes
106—John Sprungman
110-111—Lynn Walters
112 top—Michael Eckerman
    bottom—Lynn Walters
113—Michael Eckerman
118-124—Steve Magers
125—Lynn Walters
128—Steve Magers
132—Paul Sturges
136—Michael Eckerman
140 top—Ken Kern
    bottom—Bud Pratte
142—BudPratte
149—Ken Kern
152-3—Louis Pavledes
156-7—Lou Penfield
158—Lynn Walters
162—Bob Brooks
167 top left—Susanna Stewart
    top right—Lynn Walters
    bottom right—Lynn Walters
168—Lynn Walters
171—Lynn Walters
172-3—Lynn Walters
175—Lou Penfield
176—Lou Penfield
177 top—Susanna Stewart
    bottom—Steve Magers
178—Lynn Walters
180—Lynn Walters
184—Lou Penfield
187—Lynn Walters
189—Michael Eckerman
191—Michael Eckerman
back cover—Michael Eckerman

8—engraving, Abraham Bosse, Allegory of
    the Sense of Touch
other pen drawings—Steve Magers